D1483934

THE RISE OF URBAN AMERICA

THE
JUKES

Robert L. Dugdale

ARNO PRESS
&
The New York Times

NEW YORK · 1970

Reprint Edition 1970 by Arno Press Inc.

Reprinted from a copy in The University of Chicago Library

LC# 74-112542
ISBN 0-405-02451-7

THE RISE OF URBAN AMERICA
ISBN for complete set 0-405-02430-4

Manufactured in the United States of America

THE JUKES

A STUDY IN CRIME, PAUPERISM
DISEASE, AND HEREDITY

BY

ROBERT L. DUGDALE

FOURTH EDITION

WITH A FOREWORD BY
ELISHA HARRIS, M.D.
CORRESPONDING SECRETARY PRISON ASSOCIATION

AND AN INTRODUCTION BY
FRANKLIN H. GIDDINGS
PROFESSOR OF SOCIOLOGY IN COLUMBIA UNIVERSITY

G. P. PUTNAM'S SONS
NEW YORK AND LONDON
Ⲧbe 𝕶nickerbocker ℘ress

The Knickerbocker Press, New York

INTRODUCTION

"THE JUKES" has long been known as one of those important books that exert an influence out of all proportion to their bulk. It is doubtful if any concrete study of moral forces is more widely known, or has provoked more discussion, or has incited a larger number of students to examine for themselves the immensely difficult problems presented by the interaction of "heredity" with "environment."

Its achievement, moreover, is attributable to the qualities of the work itself, as much as to the unusual nature of its subject matter. It is not too much to say that when the first edition of "The Jukes" was published, it was the best example of scientific method applied to a sociological investigation. Mr. Dugdale was no closet philosopher. Neither did he depend upon data gathered for him by other men. He went himself into the field, asked his own questions, and got concrete impressions at first hand. Then, analyzing his materials and drawing inductions, he kept strictly within his data. He had no hypothesis to verify, no theoretical antagonist to throw down. His mind was intent on discovering the truth, whatever it might turn out to be, and presenting it completely, clearly, and simply.

His readers have not always been so ingenuous, certainly not always so cautious. An impression quite generally prevails that "The Jukes" is a thorough-going demonstration of "hereditary criminality," "hereditary pauperism," "hereditary degeneracy," and so on. It is nothing of the kind, and its author never made such claim for it. He undoubtedly believed in the hereditary transmission of character tendencies, as of physical traits, and here and there he points out what seem to him to be evidences of "heredity," in this sense, in the "Jukes" blood. But he is ever careful to say "seemingly," or "apparently," or otherwise to warn the reader that the conclusion is tentative. Far from believing that heredity is fatal, Mr. Dugdale was profoundly convinced that "environment" can be relied on to modify, and ultimately to eradicate even such deep-rooted and widespreading growths of vice and crime as the "Jukes" group exemplified.

Since Mr. Dugdale's studies came to a too early end the whole subject of heredity has undergone re-examination at the hands of biologists. Notions that satisfied Mr. Darwin have profoundly been modified by Weismann's contention that acquired characteristics are not transmissible, and by the discovery of the Mendelian law. No scientific man of good standing would now venture to affirm that we know enough about human heredity to justify the social reformer in basing any very radical practical program of social reform upon biological conclusions. We can only say that *probably* heredity is a fateful factor in the moral, and therefore in the social, realm, but that we need an immense amount of patient research to determine exactly what it is, and what it does.

The incontrovertible conclusion that Mr. Dugdale's investigations establish, then, is this: The factor of "heredity," whatever it may be, and whether great or small, always has the coefficient, "environment," and if bad personal antecedents are reinforced by neglect, indecent domestic arrangements, isolation from the disturbing and stimulating influences of a vigorous civilization, and, above all, if evil example is forced upon the child from his earliest infancy, the product will inevitably be an extraordinary high percentage of pauperism, vice, and crime. Two or three rather important tentative conclusions are: Illegitimacy as such does not invariably entail viciousness or criminality in descendants; crime is correlated with the crossing of vicious blood with a more vigorous outside strain; pauperism is correlated with close inbreeding of a vicious and weakened strain.

"The Jukes" has long been out of print, to the great regret of all strictly scientific students of sociology and social economy. The publishers render a service to the cause of right thinking and sound teaching in bringing out a new edition.

FRANKLIN H. GIDDINGS.

COLUMBIA UNIVERSITY, *July 20, 1910.*

PREFACE TO THIRD EDITION.

THE object of issuing these *essays* is to invite criticism, if the subjects and their treatment entitle them to notice. They are purely tentative, the results of two special inquiries, the first of County Jails in 1874, the last of State Prisons in 1875, ordered by resolution of the Prison Association of New York.

"The Jukes" is a pseudonyme used to protect from aspersion worthy members of the family therein studied, and for convenience of treatment, to reduce the forty-two family names included in the lineage to one generic application. An author who, under such circumstances, puts forth a work requiring great precision of statement and freedom from preconceived bias, is bound to state:

First: the reason for the inquiry,—Sig. M. BELTRANI-SCALIA, Inspector of Prisons in Italy, asking what is crime in those who commit it? says: "Until we shall have studied crime in its perpetrators and in all its relations and different aspects, we will never be able to discover the best means to prevent or correct it, nor can we say that penitentiary science has made any great progress. Convicts must be studied in their outward manifestations, because, by examining all the surrounding circumstances, we shall discover what we aim at—truth. Leaving aside all abstract speculations and uncertain theories, it is requisite that in moral science, we should follow the same path that has been so advantageously taken in the study of natural science * * * because moral facts, as well as those which are called natural facts, have a cause so to be." After going over the history of the discussions on penitentiary reform for the last fifty years, he adds: "The study of the prisoner is the greatest need still felt after so many years of toil and debate. We have just reached that point where we should have commenced, because, after so much labor, we have only reached an empty space."

Second: the authority on which his statements rest;—These are for genealogies, intemperance and social habits, the testimony of old residents who have known the older branches, of relatives, of employers, of records and of officials. For diseases: physicians and poor-house records. For pauperism: the poor-house records. For out-door relief: the books of town poor-masters. For crimes: the records of the county clerk's office, the sheriff's books and prison registers. No other testimony has been accepted for crime and pauperism except that of official records; and as many of these could not be obtained, the facts in these respects are greatly understated.

Third: the manner in which the facts have been gathered.—In the genealogy of the "Jukes," the method employed has been to avoid method lest I should unconsciously fall into the error of being dominated by fore-gone conclusions. I have therefore merely recorded in the order of their occurrence *all* the authenticated facts of each life brought to my notice, giving the age at which they took place, so that the sequence of phe-nomena could be distinctly traced and the nature of the accompanying environment be noted, to enable us to compare generation with generation and measure the relative importance of heredity and environment in the shaping of individual careers. Difficulties, most of them surmountable, prevented my including many topographical, political, social, economic, hygienic and other factors which belong to the inquiry, and this defective-ness in the range of facts presented precludes my offering any conclusions authoritatively ; but the accumulated testimony illustrates the application and justification of the treatment of the subject discussed.

The second paper is the result of an examination of felon convicts on a very ample schedule, covering their physical, mental, moral and ances-tral traits to test the accuracy of what purports to be the public records of crime in this State ; to establish the value of expert work in making a minute census of the prison population, including the trustworthiness of convict testimony, and to lay the basis for a wider and more thorough ap-plication of the method of research pursued in the study of the " Jukes." The effort to trace back the genealogy in these cases was sufficiently extended to fulfil some of the conditions of the present investigation, but no exhaustive prosecution of the subject was pushed, as no adequate means were at hand to that end. Thus, even the limited number of sched-ules (233) of criminals gathered remain in hand, till adequate authority and means shall warrant the further prosecution of the research to positive conclusions.

I am informed that $28,000 was raised in two days to purchase a rare collection of antique jewelry and bronzes recently discovered in classic ground, forty feet below the *débris*. I do not hear of as many pence being offered to fathom the *débris* of our civilization, however rich the yield. I do not complain that men of wealth expend their means as they prefer, but it seems not captious that I should wish crime and pauperism were as rare as the exhumed treasures, that they might arouse equal zeal for deep research. There is, perhaps, yet hope, for these subjects have a claim to far greater antiquity inasmuch as they reach back to time immemorial, which assuredly antedates the bronzes.

R. L. D.

New York, May, 1877.

FOREWORD.

The line of inquiry pursued by Mr. DUGDALE and briefly recited in these pages, will aid all persons searching out the preventable sources of crime and endeavoring to repress it. Whoever carefully investigates the history of individual offenders and traces out the careers of typical groups of the offending classes, will recognize the practical bearings of this definite and comprehensive study of the physical, mental and social circumstances under which they are nurtured.

A departure downward, from virtue to vice and crime, is possible in the career of any youth; but the number of well-born and well-trained children who thus fall is exceedingly small. Habitual criminals spring almost exclusively from degenerating stocks; their youth is spent amid the degrading surroundings of physical and social defilement, with only a flickering of the redeeming influence of virtuous aspiration. The career of offenders so trained, at last becomes a reckless warfare against society; and when the officers of justice overtake them and consign them to prisons, the habits of vicious thought and criminal action have acquired the strength and quality of instincts.

The correctional discipline which is sought for in our prisons and reformatories, although a necessary public duty, is vastly more expensive and unsatisfactory than the application of preventive measures would be. These latter must be adjusted within the bosom of society, and will be effective just in proportion to the intelligence, health and active virtues of the people.

In the progress of medical science the close study of healthful as well as morbid conditions has resulted in defining the rules of hygiene, which treats of the prevention and extinction of the causes of disease. In like manner a search into the sources of the habitually criminal classes reveals that out of the same social

3

soil from which spring the majority of the criminals, there, also, chiefly grow up the vagrants and paupers—the ignorant, vicious and incapable. The prevention of crime requires the same comprehensive knowledge and treatment of the sanitary and physiological, the domestic and social, the educational, industrial and religious interests of the common people, as must be applied to prevent diseases and their entailment. Mr. DUGDALE's inquiry into the lineage of perhaps the largest family of criminals and paupers ever studied, and his subsequent prosecution of a similar investigation in the State prisons, are well designed to establish a sound basis for the effectual repression of the causes of crime; for in all that relates to human society and the wants of mankind, " the determination of evils is the first step of their remedies."

Rarely has such a patient and philosophical inquirer as Mr. DUGDALE penetrated the social *hades* of the dangerous classes, and in their own abodes so photographed them as vagabonds, as offenders, as the out-door poor of a country, as felons and mis-creants,—that their unvarnished picture is recognized by all who ever saw these " Jukes" or any of their kind. It is a duty for me to bear testimony to the scrupulous and exhaustive methods of investigation adopted by Mr. DUGDALE in his researches into the physical and social condition of this great group, which, as well in ancestry as hereditary out-come, presents a complete physio-logical and moral record of the degeneracy which fills prisons and almshouses and mocks the almoner of out-door and way-side relief. A more enlightened student of social conditions than the author of this record has probably never before set about investigating the natural history of crime and pauperism; and as the individual and family histories which he gleaned and grouped in this inves-tigation were laid before me progressively verified, and his inquiries were made under official appointment by the Prison Association, as one of its executive committee, every assurance is given respecting the correctness of this study of ruined generations.

ELISHA HARRIS, M. D.,
Corres. Sec'y. Prison Association of N. Y.

THE JUKES

I

THE JUKES.

A RECORD AND STUDY OF THE RELATIONS OF CRIME, PAUPERISM, DISEASE AND HEREDITY.

In July, 1874, the New York Prison Association having deputed me to visit thirteen of the county jails of this State and report thereupon, I made a tour of inspection in pursuance of that appointment. No specially striking cases of criminal careers, traceable through several generations, presented themselves till —— county was reached. Here, however, were found six persons, under four family names, who turned out to be blood relations in some degree. The oldest, a man of fifty-five, was waiting trial for receiving stolen goods ; his daughter, aged eighteen, held as witness against him ; her uncle, aged forty-two, burglary in the first degree ; the illegitimate daughter of the latter's wife, aged twelve years, upon which child the latter had attempted rape, to be sent to the reformatory for vagrancy ; and two brothers in another branch of the family, aged respectively nineteen and fourteen, accused of an assault with intent to kill, they having maliciously pushed a child over a high cliff and nearly killed him. Upon trial the oldest was acquitted, though the goods stolen were found in his house, his previous good character saving him ; the guilt belonged to his brother-in-law, the man aged forty-two, above mentioned, who was living in the house. This brother-in-law is an illegitimate child, an habitual criminal and the son of an unpunished and cautious thief. He had two brothers and one sister, all of whom are thieves, the sister being the contriver of crime, they its executors. The daughter of this woman, the girl aged eighteen above mentioned, testified at the trial which resulted in convicting her uncle and procuring his sentence for twenty years to State prison, that she was forced to join him in his last foray ; that he had loaded her with the booty, and beat her on the journey home, over two miles, because she lagged under the load. When this girl was released, her family in jail and thus left without a home, she was forced to make her lodging in a brothel on the outskirts of the city. Next morning she applied to the judge to be recommitted to prison " for protection " against specified carnal outrages required of her and submitted to. She has since been sent to the house of refuge. Of the two boys, one was discharged by the Grand Jury ; the other was tried and received five years' imprisonment in Sing Sing.

These six persons belonged to a long lineage, reaching back to the early colonists, and had intermarried so slightly with the emigrant population of the old world that they may be called a strictly American family. They had lived in the same locality for generations, and were so despised by the reputable community that their family name *had come to be used generically as a term of reproach.*

That this was deserved became manifest on slight inquiry. It was found that out of twenty-nine males, in ages ranging from fifteen to seventy-five, the immediate blood relations of these six persons, seventeen of them were criminals, or fifty-eight per cent ; while fifteen were convicted of some degree of offense, and received seventy-one years of sentence. Fuller details are shown in the table opposite, the name " Juke " standing for the blood relations of those found in the jail, the capital " X " for relations by marriage or cohabitation.

The crimes and misdemeanors they committed were assault and battery, assault with intent to kill, murder, attempt at rape, petit larceny, grand larceny, burglary, forgery, cruelty to animals. With these facts in hand, it was thought wise to extend the investigation to other branches of the family, and explore it more thoroughly.

The sheriff communicated the names of two gentlemen—lifelong residents of the county, one of them 84 years old and for many

TABLE I.

Showing Crime in the Illegitimate Branch of Ada Juke.

	Total number of adults.	Adult males.	Adult females.	Number of male criminals.	Number of convicted male criminals.	Years of sentence.
Juke blood..............................	49	29	20	17	15	71
X blood	32	16	16	5	5	8¼
Total....................	81	45	36	22	20	79¼

years town physician—who gave me the genealogies of many of the branches of this family, with details of individual biographies. This opened up so large a field of study, that I then had no idea of its extent and still less of the unexpected results which a subsequent analysis disclosed.

Method of study defined.—Having brought back a very incomplete genealogical tree including 100 persons, Dr. Elisha Harris, the Corresponding Secretary of the Association, urged me to push the inquiry, and I returned to the country to resume the search. The facts in hand both suggested and necessitated a modification of the conventional methods employed by statisticians in anthropological studies. Social and moral statistics include the science and the art of registering, in categories, such analogous social facts as are expressible in numerical terms. There are two forms which are in vogue, Positive Statistics and Conjectural Statistics.

Positive Statistics, of which the census of population is the best illustration, merely enumerates facts that are congruous, co-ordinates them so as to reduce them to a common measure for purposes of comparison to analogous facts as to quantity, frequency, time and place, being careful not to alter them by the artifices of mathematical estimates. The basis of its method is experimental, the process of its teachings is by exposition, and scientifically it is the simplest

1*

and safest. For these reasons I have given it the preference. In collating its materials it is liable to a fundamental error, that of comparing similar facts which are not identical because they do not occur under similar conditions, as where the frequency of crime among men is compared to that among women, using official records, when we know that the law and the administration of the law treat women with more leniency than men. But Positive Statistics does not explain the causes or the consequences of facts, therefore conclusions drawn from its figures are inferential and may lead to mistaking coincidences for correlations, as where it is concluded that because criminals show a larger percentage of illiteracy than the average of the community, therefore illiteracy is a cause of crime.

Conjectural Statistics consists of Political Arithmetic and the Theory of Probabilities. The first is a method of computing estimates of unknown facts by means of known ones, using the rule of three or other mathematical devices for that purpose. For instance, knowing what proportion of paupers to population there is in one county it assumes that all the other counties in a State have the same ratio of pauperism, while, by actual count, some of them have a higher and some a lower ratio. The Theory of Probabilities is a special application of the above to calculate the chance which a given event has of occurring or not occurring in a given number of times, and requires a profound knowledge of mathematics. Life insurance is based on the probability that, say out of a thousand persons born, a given number will die within one, two or more years. But it cannot tell us which person will die at any time, although it can tell us how many will survive after any given term of years. Its essential process is to reduce all facts to an average, and in doing so it substitutes an abstract mathematical entity of uniform quality and degree in place of the actual concrete facts. The dangers of this method are that facts of the same nature, but differing in intensity, are classed together when their effects are not distributive. Thus heat, which, at one degree warms, at another withers, at another devastates, produces at each extreme effects which are diametrically opposite, but which are nevertheless made compensative by reduction to an average and appear as if they were identical to the mean from which they both differ. It also loses points of initial divergence (essential elements in the study of causation) which, with slight deflection at first, produce, when followed through successive removes to their cumulation, ultimate results not classifiable under the same head. A similiar criticism may be made as to diverse contributive causes producing similar effects.

The study of causation is a mental process which is not statistics, but in which the latter are a great assistance.

In the study of the pathology of social disorders, many of them resting primarily upon organic disease of body or mind, and therefore requiring a critical exploring and analysis of the causes and consequences of constitutional habits, statistics could be used only as an adjunct. Therefore the minute study of individual lives has been made the leading feature, hoping it would contribute to a just discrimination, link by link, of the essential from the accidental elements of social movement which occur in the sequence of phenomena, the distribution of social growth and decay, and the tendency, direction and significance of social eccentricities.

By a modification of the original schedule prepared by the Corresponding Secretary, adding the element of time and the order of events, it was easily adapted to the objective point of the present inquiry, the study of the sequence of phenomena as set forth in criminal and pauper careers, to discover if there are laws in their evolution, knowing which, it becomes easy to institute measures adequate to their control.

Observation discloses that any given series of social phenomena —as honest childhood, criminal maturity and pauper old age, which sometimes occur in the life of a single individual—may be stretched over several generations, each step being removed from the other by a generation, and in some cases, by two. Consequently, the nature of the investigation necessitated the study of families through successive generations, to master the full sequence of phenomena and include the entire facts embraced in the two main branches of inquiry into which the subject necessarily divides itself : THE HEREDITY that fixes the organic characteristics of the individual, and THE ENVIRONMENT which affects modifications in that heredity.

It reduces the method of study, then, to one of historico-biographical synthesis united to statistical analysis, enabling us to estimate the cumulative effects of any condition which has operated through successive generations : heredity giving us those elements of character which are derived from the parent as a birthright, environment all the events and conditions occurring after birth which have contributed to shape the individual career or deflect its primitive tendency.

Heredity and environment, then, are the parallels between which the questions of crime and public dependence and their judicious treatment extend : the objective point is to determine how much of each results from heredity, how much from environment. The answer to these determines the limits of possibility in amending vicious lives, and the scrutiny will reveal some of the methods which the present organization of society automatically sets in motion, which, without conscious design nevertheless convert harmful careers into useful ones. The discovery of such spontaneous social activities will furnish models to be followed in dealing with the unbalanced.

Now heredity takes two leading forms that need to be contrasted ; consanguinity and crossing, each presenting modified results. Environment may judiciously be divided into two main branches : the surroundings which throw men into criminal careers and keep them in such ; the surroundings which rescue them from criminal careers and keep them out. These two natural divisions, with their subdivisions, form the key-note to the present inquiry. A reference to the four charts contained in this *essay* will show how the events in the life of the parent are reproduced in the career of the child, and allows a strict comparison to be made between the life of the latter and that of his generation or his posterity, so that any characteristic which is hereditary will thus be revealed. On the other hand, the environment of each generation can be studied, the changes in that environment can be noted, and the results of the same can be ascertained.

Taking a general survey of the characteristics of the " Jukes " and for the purpose of convenient illustration, the leading facts are grouped in the following diagram which, however, is not offered as a generalization.

CONSANGUINITY.

Crime.		Fornication.		Pauperism.
Prostitution.			Illegitimacy.	
Exhaustion.			Intemperance.	
Disease.			Extinction.	

NOT CONSANGUINEOUS.

In other words, *fornication*, either consanguineous or not, is the backbone of their habits, flanked on one side by *pauperism*, on the other by *crime*. The secondary features are *prostitution*, with its complement of *bastardy*, and its resultant neglected and miseducated childhood ; *exhaustion*, with its complement *intemperance* and its resultant unbalanced minds ; and *disease* with its complement *extinction*.

The habitat of the " Jukes."—The ancestral breeding-spot of this family nestles along the forest-covered margin of five lakes, so rocky as to be at some parts inaccessible. It may be called one of the crime cradles of the State of New York ; for in subsequent examinations of convicts in the different State prisons, a number of them were found to be the descendants of families equivalent to the " Jukes," and emerging from this nest. Most of the ancestors were squatters upon the soil, and in some instances have become owners by tax-title or by occupancy. They lived in log or stone houses similar to slave-hovels, all ages, sexes, relations and strangers " bunking" indiscriminately. One form of this bunking has been described to me. During the winter the inmates lie on the floor strewn with straw or rushes like so many radii to the hearth, the embers of the fire forming a centre towards which their feet focus for warmth. This proximity, where not producing illicit relations, must often have evolved an atmosphere of suggestiveness fatal to habits of chastity. To this day some of the " Jukes" occupy the self-same shanties built nearly a century ago. The essential features of the habitat have remained stationary, and the social habits seem to survive in conformity to the persistence of the domiciliary environment. I have seen rude shelters made of boughs covered with sod, or the refuse slabs of saw mills set slanting against ledges of rock and used in the summer as abodes, the occupants bivouacing much as gypsies. Others of the habitations have two rooms, but so firmly has habit established modes of living, that, nevertheless, they often use but one congregate dormitory. Sometimes I found an overcrowding so close it suggested that these dwellings were the country equivalents of city tenement houses. Domesticity is impossible. The older girls, finding no privacy within a home overrun with younger brothers and sisters, purchase privacy at the risk of prudence, and the night rambles through woods and tangles end, too often, in illegitimate offspring. During the last thirty years, however, the establishment of factories has brought about the building of houses better suited to secure domesticity, and with this change alone, an accompanying change in personal habits is being introduced, which would otherwise be impossible.

The origin of the Stock of the " Jukes."—Between the years 1720 and 1740 was born a man who shall herein be called Max. He was a descendant of the early Dutch settlers, and lived much as the backwoodsmen upon our frontiers now do. He is described as " a hunter and fisher, a hard drinker, jolly and companionable, averse to steady toil," working hard by spurts and idling by turns, becoming blind in his old age, and entailing his blindness upon his children and grandchildren. He had a numerous progeny, some of them almost certainly illegitimate. Two of his sons married two out of six sisters (called " Jukes " in these pages) who were born between the year 1740 and 1770, but whose parentage has not been absolutely ascertained. The probability is they were not full sisters, that some, if not all of them, were illegitimate. The family name, in two cases, is obscure, which accords with the supposition that at least two of the women were half-sisters to the other four, the legitimate daughters bearing the family name, the illegitimate keeping either the mother's name or adopting that of the reputed father. Five of these women in the first generation were married ; the sixth one it has been impossible to trace, for she moved out of the county. Of the five that are known, three have had illegitimate children before marriage. One who is called in these pages Ada Juke, but who is better known to the public as "Margaret, the mother of criminals," had one bastard son, who is the progenitor of the distinctively criminal line. Another sister had two illegitimate sons, who appear to have had no children. A third sister had four, three boys and one girl, the three oldest children being mulattoes, and the youngest— a boy—white. The fourth sister is reputed chaste, while no information could be gathered respecting the fifth in this respect, but she was the mother of one of the distinctively pauperized lines and married one of the sons of Max. The progeny of these five has been traced with more or less exactness through five generations, thus making the total heredity which has been enrolled stretch over seven generations, if we count Max as the first. The number of descendants registered includes 540 individuals who are related by blood to the Jukes, and 169 by marriage or cohabitation ; in all, 709 persons of all ages, alive and dead. The aggregate of this lineage reaches probably 1,200 persons, but the dispersions that have occurred at different times have prevented the following up and enumeration of many of the lateral branches.

Discrimination of Stocks.—To distinguish those who are directly descended from these five sisters, they will be spoken of as belonging to the "Juke blood," because it is the line of their blood which has been traced, it being the most important as a study of heredity, the male lineage being considered subordinate. As the heredity of those who enter the family by marriage is in most instances uncertain, these persons will be spoken of generically as "the blood of X," or "the X blood." In order to trace the relationships more easily, the five sisters will be called, respectively, "Ada," "Bell," "Clara," "Delia," "Effie," the names beginning with the first five letters of the alphabet, which letter, in the text and appended charts, will be used instead of the full name. Individuals outside the line will be marked by an X.

How to read the Charts.—The children resulting from any given marriage will contain all the letters which represent their ancestral derivation, each child being numbered according to the order of its birth as nearly as could be learned. Thus turning to chart I., facing page 15, in the first line in the column headed "generation three, you will find " (1) b. m. A. 70 $\times$ (6) l. f. B.," which would mean that the first child of Ada, a bastard male, aged seventy at death, married the sixth legitimate female child of Bell, age unknown. Passing to the next generation we should get " (1) l. m. A. B. $\times$ f. X.," the first child, a legitimate male of A. and B., married a female whose antecedents are unknown. Passing down to the next generation we should get " (2) l. f. A. B. X. = (1) b. m. E. X. X.," which means the second child, a legitimate female, of A. B. and X., cohabits with the first child, an illegitimate male, of E. X. and X. Other abbreviations will be found explained on the charts.

Consanguinity and Crossing.—In surveying the whole family, as it is the mapped out in the Charts, I find groups which may be considered distinctively industrious, distinctively criminal, distinctively pauper, and specifically diseased. These features run along lines of descent so that you can follow them from generation to generation, the breaks in the line at certain points indicating with great precision the modifying effects of disease, training, or fortuitous circumstance which have intervened and changed the current of the career.

A glance at table II., which epitomizes in a very general way the details contained in the larger charts, shows these distinctions with measurable accuracy, and helps us to some conclusions :

Tentative Inductions.—1. Boys preponderate in the illegitimate lines.

2. Girls preponderate in the intermarried branches.

3. Lines of intermarriage between " Jukes " show a minimum of crime.

4. Pauperism preponderates in the consanguineous lines.

5. In the main, crime begins in progeny where " Juke " crosses X blood.

6. The illegitimate lines have chiefly married into X.

7. Crime preponderates in the illegitimate lines.

8. The apparent anomaly presents itself, that the illegitimate criminal lines show collateral branches which are honest and industrious. When we come to the study of crime and honesty, and their relation to character and environment, we shall find an explanation of this apparent inconsistency.

TABLE II.

Second generation.	Third generation.	Fourth generation.	Fifth generation.	REMARKS.
Ada, harlot before marriage.	A. ⋈ B., no crime *.	A. B. ⋈ X., crime......	A. B. X., crime.......	Preponderance of males } Bastard line.
	A. ⋈ C., no crime......	A. B. ⋈ D. X., reputable	A. B. D. X., reputable.	Semi-successful........}
	A. ⋈ D., no crime	A. C. ⋈ X., no crime...	A. C. B. C., no crime..	Legitimate. Preponderance of girls.
	A. ⋈ X., no crime	A. D. ⋈ X., no crime...	No crime	Legitimate. Distinct:vely pauper line.
		A. X. ⋈ E. X., pauper...	A. X. E. X., pauper....	
Bell, harlot before marriage.	B. ⋈ X., no crime	B. X. ⋈ X., reputable	Honest	Successful branch } Bastard line.
		B. X. ⋈ X., crime......	B. X. X., crime	Criminal branch }
	B. ⋈ C., no crime......	B. C. ⋈ X., no crime...	....	Legitimate.
Clara, of good repute	C. ⋈ X., not traced	....	....	Legitimate. Not traced.
	See A. ⋈ C. and B. ⋈ C.	....	....	Legitimate.
Delia, harlot before marriage	D. ⋈ X., no crime	D. X. ⋈ X., crime......	D. X. X., crime.......	Legitimate.
		D. X. ⋈ B. C., no crime	D. X. B. C., no crime ..	Bastard line.
Effie, reputation unknown.	E. = X*...............	E. X. ⋈ X., crime......	Not traced...........	Bastard line and barren.
	E. ⋈ X., no crime			Legitimate.

*Explanation, ⋈ Married, = Cohabiting with.

B

Harlotry.—The distinctive tendency of the Juke family is dis‧
played in the statistical exhibit herein presented ; for the most nota‧
ble figures are those that relate to harlotry and bastardy.

The term harlotry in these pages will be used generically, includ‧
ing all degrees of impudicity.   Inasmuch as the English language
possesses no word to distinguish women who professionally sell
themselves from those who have made lapses through imprudence or
even passion when they have recovered themselves and led subse‧
quently reputable lives, I shall use the word harlot to mean the
lesser degree, while prostitute will be applied to the professional
debauchee.

In the following table all girls of 14 are included among the
marriageable women, because there are at least two mothers under
15 years of age, one being only twelve.

TABLE III.

Harlotry in the " Juke " blood.

	Gen. 2.	Gen. 3.	Gen. 4.	Gen. 5.	Gen. 6.	Totals.
Number of marriageable women..	5	16	39	90	12	162
Aggregate of harlotry	3	6	27	44	4	84
Percentage of harlotry..........	60	37.24	69.23	48.88	38.33	52.40

The variation of percentages in the different generations is be‧
cause the sources of information have not been exhausted.   In the
second generation we have a very small basis for calculating per‧
centages, while in the sixth generation the 12 girls are so young that
the percentage is not fully developed.   A complete account would,
no doubt, make them approximate more nearly, increasing the per‧
centage of harlotry for the total.   How enormous it is, amounting
to a distinctive social feature, is demonstrated on comparison with
the average prostitution in cities, which has been estimated by good
authorities as 1.66 per cent, or one woman in every sixty.   These
figures are probably too low for harlotry in the community.   Sup‧
posing them to be 1.80 per cent, we find harlotry over twenty-nine

times more frequent with the Juke women than in the average of the community.

Making a comparison between the women of the " Juke " and the X blood, we find :

" Jukes "—marriageable women, 162 ; harlots, 84 . percentage, 52. 40.
X blood—marriageable women, 67 ; harlots, 28 : percentage, 41. 76.

Having the figures that establish the sexual habits of the female " Jukes," and their accompanying tendency, we take up the question in its details. In the following study of licentiousness, the lives of the women have, by preference, been chosen, because the maternity is more easily established by testimony, is much more significant of the social condition of the whole class, and more profoundly affects the next generation.

Below is given a table in which the marriageable female posterity of Clara, who was chaste, is compared to the marriageable female posterity of Ada, a harlot, divided respectively as to the legitimate and illegitimate branches. In this table the children of Clara are

TABLE IV.

Showing percentages of harlotry.

	Clara's, who have married outside the Ada and Bell lines.	Clara's, total number, who have married into A and B.	Ada's legitimate.	Ada's illegitimate.	Average of "Juke" women, as by Table III.
Number of marriageable women......	18	64	36	20	
Unascertained	2	6	6	2	
Reputable	8	19	6	4	
Harlots before marriage............	3	5	5	8	
Harlots after marriage	2	10	4	1	
Prostitutes	3	24	15	5	
Total harlotry......................	8	39	24	14	
Percentage of harlotry to total women.	44.44	60.93	66.66	70	52.40

divided into two classes—the first column being those who married into X ; the second, the total number of her children, including those who intermarried with the children of Ada and Bell. The percentages show a progressive increase as you pass from left to right,

the first column showing a lower percentage than that of the average of the "Jukes," the others increasing as you proceed to consanguineous marriages of Clara's stock with the children of Ada
and Bell, to the legitimate children of Ada, to the illegitimate children of Ada. From this point of view it would seem that chastity
and profligacy are hereditary characteristics, possible of entailment.

This table illustrates how pure statistics may lead into the error
of mistaking a coincidence for a correlation, for the figures appear
to demonstrate the force of heredity, the chaste mother bearing a
progeny more chaste than the unchaste mother, and the legitimate
branch of the unchaste mother being more chaste than the illegitimate branch. To study out the causation we trace several of the
most striking lines of harlotry, get elements which are not to be
found in the table, because that gives only an average that obliterates
extremes which teach lessons that the mean conceals. We shall
then see how far to modify first impressions on closer analysis.

Case 1. Taking up the legitimate branch of Ada, which intermarried into Bell and Clara (chart II.), we follow the heredity of
legitimacy in lines 6, 8 and 10, generation 5. They are three
sisters, children of a legitimate father, B. C., and a chaste and legitimate mother, A. C., whose mother C. (gen. 3, following the mother's
side) was a chaste and legitimate daughter of Clara, who was chaste.
Going back to the father (gen. 4), we find his mother (gen. 3) was a
chaste, legitimate daughter of Clara. Both parents, therefore, of
generation four, were of chaste descent on the mother's side. Thus,
the original characteristic of chastity seems to have descended from
Clara through two branches, A. and B., and cumulated in the three
sisters under consideration. Further ; we find, in line 7, the sister
of the above three to be a prostitute, and in going back upon the
heredity, we find in gen. 4 that the father's father was the licentious,
though legitimate, son of Ada, a harlot, and on the mother's side
(gen. 4), the father was the legitimate son of Bell, a prostitute. According to the law of heredity, it is a logical deduction to make,
that line 7 has reverted to the ancestral types on the unchaste
side of both parents. Respecting this case, very little reliable information has been gathered about the environment, but it must be
noted that the mother in generation four was one of seven sisters,

one of whom was idiotic, and no doubt licentious, and five others, harlots or prostitutes, one of them keeping a brothel ; while, on the father's (see chart III., gen. 4, line 37), there was one sister who also kept a brothel. Whether this pair removed from the vicinity of their relations has not been learned, and what were the other particulars of their career are unknown. This case looks more like one of pure heredity than any that has been traced.

Case 2. Taking line 13, and following the heredity, we have (gen. 6) two illegitimate children of a white woman. One of them was a mulatto girl, who died at one year old of syphilis, whose mother (gen. 5) was a bastard prostitute, afflicted with the same disease, whose mother (gen. 4) was a prostitute afflicted likewise in the constitutional form, inherited from her licentious father, whose mother, Ada, was a harlot.

Now for the environment. The infant girl who died was conceived by the roadside, and born in the poor-house. Its mother (gen. 5) was a vagrant child, her mother having no home for her. So neglected was she, that at seven years she was committed to the county jail for a misdemeanor. She was idle, disgustingly dirty, and for that reason could get no place as a servant, and as she must live, fell into the practice of prostitution. Her half-sister also had an illegitimate child, while other relations and acquaintances gave the example of profligacy. Her mother (gen. 4) was married twice—then cohabited with the man who became this girl's father, and when he went to the war in 1863 and deserted her, she followed the example of her other four prostitute sisters, one of whom kept a brothel. Going back to the father (gen. 3) we find him a soldier in the war of 1812, very licentious, whose two harlot sisters married mulattoes. As this was at a time when slavery existed in this State, the social condition under which this consorting took place is significant.

We have here an environment in three generations which corresponds to the heredity ; this environment forming an example to the younger generation which must have been sufficient, without heredity, to stimulate licentious practices.

Case 3. Turning to the illegitimate branch of Ada (chart I.), trace the heredity of legitimacy in lines 40 and 41 (gen. 6), two

girls who are legitimate, whose mothers (gen. 5) were sisters, chaste
and legitimate, whose father and mother (gen. 4) were legitimate
and chaste, whose mother (gen. 3, following the father's side) was
legitimate and chaste, whose mother was Ada, a harlot. Following the mother's side (gen. 4), her mother was a legitimate child of
Delia, a harlot. Here the heredity seems not entailed.

Now for the environment. The three sisters of generation 5
are industrious women, who work at tailoring, and are described by
their employer as always reliable, and doing their work by the time
promised. The oldest brother, who is a mason, has amassed some
$2,000 at his trade, which he has invested in a house and lot. He
is steady and industrious. Going back to generation 4, we find the
father a mason, tolerably industrious, who separated himself from
his brothers and sisters, the sum total of whose environment may
be thus expressed: Three sisters and one sister-in-law, prostitutes,
and the other sister-in-law a brothel keeper; of the four men, one
brother kept a brothel, the other was a quarrelsome drunkard, one
brother-in-law was an habitual thief, who trained his sons to crime,
another served two years in State prison for forgery. This pair
thus measurably protected themselves and their progeny from the
environment of eight contaminating persons, all immediate relatives,
whose lives were, with few exceptions, quite profligate. Going
back to generation 3, we have no account of the environment, save
that there was no prostitution, while at the head of the line, we
find Ada on one branch and Bell on the other.

In this case we again note that, in the fourth and fifth generations, while the heredity is mainly of the type of chasity, the environment has also been favorable to the same habits, but in generation 3 the characteristics of harlotry in Ada and Bell are not
reproduced as we might expect if heredity were the controlling
element in determining the career. If the history of the environment of that generation could only be obtained, it would, perhaps,
explain the interruption in the entailment.

Case 4. Taking line 35, chart I., we have (gen. 7) an illegitimate
child, whose mother (gen. 6) was a prostitute, whose mother (gen.
5) was a bastard prostitute, whose mother (gen. 4) was a harlot,
whose father (gen. 3) was a bastard son of Ada, a harlot, while his

wife (gen. 3) was the legitimate daughter of Bell, a prostitute. Going back and following up from the father in generation 4, we find his father the illegitimate son of Bell.

Parallel to this we lay the story of the environment. The mother of this child in the seventh generation is the daughter of a prostitute, who kept a brothel when that daughter was only ten years old. It is stated by one of the poor-masters that, upon one occasion, the daughter applied to him for out-door relief to maintain the above child. She made a charge of bastardy against a certain man, whom the poor-master was called upon, in virtue of his office, to prosecute for the maintenance of the child. The case was lost, and after the trial was over in the magistrate's office, the male witnesses adjourned to a neighboring bar-room where, for a few dollars, the mother caused her daughter to retract the story publicly. Going back to the fourth generation, the testimony as to environment is not so complete, only that the father was dissolute, and that the example of the other sisters no doubt had an influence in blunting the sense of purity, while, in the two generations farther back, the testimony is not sufficiently definite for the purposes of the present argument.

Here, again, environment is in the line of heredity.

Case 5. The most striking case of all is line 23, chart I., for in it we find bastardy in every link but one. In generation 7 is found an illegitimate girl six years old, whose mother (gen. 6) was an illegitimate prostitute, whose mother (gen. 5) was a harlot, whose mother (gen. 4) was illegitimate, married to a husband (gen. 4) whose father (gen. 3) was illegitimate, whose mother was Ada, a harlot.

The environment in this case stands thus : The child is the offspring of an incestuous relation between her mother when only fourteen, with her own uncle, who had served two terms in State prison, thus showing the influence of her surroundings. The mother (gen. 5) kept a brothel, and it was no doubt within its atmosphere that the girl was contaminated. Going back to generation 4 we find the parents keep a low dram-shop, which also serves on occasion as a house of assignation. As in the other cases there is no environment traced beyond.

In this again the environment runs parallel to the heredity.

Case 6. Now we take a quite different case, where the heredity and the environment have coincided up to a certain age, and yet the career of harlotry has not been run. Follow line 30, chart I., to generation 5, is a girl, the sister of the woman in case 5, mentioned above, who kept a brothel and whose heredity has been traced. Substantially, the environment was the same as that of her two sisters who were both prostitutes. How closely she followed them up to her fifteenth year is shown by the fact that in 1861 we find her, together with her sister, arrested for vagrancy and locked up in the county jail for two days. At this point, however, the environment changes. She marries a German, a cement burner, a steady, industrious, plodding man, settles down into a home, brings legitimate children into the world and takes the position of a reputable woman. In this case it is plain that the change in the environment has supplanted the tendency of the heredity. The case now is to be watched to see if, in spite of the environment of a reputable home, the daughter of this woman, now 12 years of age, will revert to the ancestral characteristics, and change what now seems to be an argument in favor of the potency of environment into an argument proving the prepotency of heredity.

If prostitution were merely a private vice, the bad effects of which were confined to the individual practicing it, it would be a matter of only secondary moment, but the bearing which the subject has upon the increase and perpetuation of crime arises from the fact that it leads to neglected and miseducated childhood, which develops adults without sense of moral obligation, without self-respect and without a proper desire for the approbation of reputable people.

Looking over the aggregate of harlotry—84—we find 18 of the women subsequently married. Inasmuch as in this 84 are included a number of girls under 20 some of whom will yet marry, it would be fair to estimate at 22 the number who will marry and avoid a prostitute career, which would be 26.19 per cent of the total harlotry, or over one-fourth, and this, apparently in the face of the force of heredity. The old truth here appears that the tendency of marriage is to extinguish prostitution. When we take into consideration case 6, line 30, who became a reputable wife in spite of her heredity and of her environment by simply being married at 15 years of age, the question presents itself whether early marriage among the class we are studying, is not the spontaneous and, therefore, most efficient means of reducing the crop of criminals and paupers.

Harlotry, compared to Pauperism and Crime.—As respects pauperism : 1st. Of males receiving out-door relief there are over 20 per cent, of females a little under 13 per cent ; receiving alms-house relief, males nearly 13 per cent, females 9½ per cent ; thus there is a preponderance of males helped by charity (see table VI.). 2d. The charts show that in the majority of cases the women receiving out-door relief, being married, merely follow the condition of their husbands. 3d. Where the women are single a large proportion of them get assistance during the child-bearing period, and only then. 4th. A number who have become widows have ceased to get relief and simultaneously taken to prostitution Thus, although the rate of wages of women is much below that of men, the application for charity is much less frequent. On examination it will be seen that, in families where the brothers are receiving relief and the sisters are not married, those sisters are many of them prostitutes.

As to crime (see table IX.), we find that while there are 34 male offenders, many of them committing very high crimes, there are only 16 females, and they committed misdemeanors in all cases but one. But on the other hand, if you look at the families in which crime is found, there, where the brothers commit crime, the sisters adopt prostitution, the fines and imprisonment of the women being not for violations of the rights of property, but mainly for offenses against public decency. The explanation is, perhaps, that the tendency of human beings is to obtain their living in the direction of least resistance according to their own views as to what that direction is, and as that direction for men of this class seems to them to be either in pauperism or in crime, the brothers enter these *vocations*. The sisters finding in prostitution a more lucrative career than pauperism, and a more safe and easy one than crime, thus avoid both in a measurable degree. Taking the illegitimate branch of Ada where the prostitution is 29 times greater than in the general community, we also find that crime among the men is 30 times greater. Taking into further consideration that the women find indulgences in a career of harlotry which their brothers can only obtain by purchase with the proceeds of theft, it is a fair inference to make that prostitution in the women is the analogue of crime and pauperism in the men, the difference in the career being only an accident of sex. The identity of the three, as distributed between the sexes, is established by finding that in this family they have a common origin, an equal ratio, and yield to the same general reformatory treatment—steady, continuous, and fatigue-producing labor.

From the consideration of the special cases detailed, we now come to formulating a few tentative inductions on the subject.

1. Harlotry may become a hereditary characteristic and be perpetuated without any specially favoring environment to call it into activity. (See case 1.)

2. In most cases the heredity is also accompanied by an environment which runs parallel to it, the two conditions giving cumulative force to a career of debauch.

3. Where there is chastity in the heredity, the same is also accompanied with an environment favorable to such habits.

4. Where the heredity and the environment are in the direction of harlotry, if the environment be changed at a sufficiently early period, the career of prostitution may be arrested and the sexual habits amended. (See case 6.)

5. That early marriage tends to extinguish harlotry.

6. That prostitution in the woman is the analogue of crime and pauperism in the man.

7. As a corollary of this last, a practical rule may be laid down to help us estimate the chances of reforming a boy who has committed his first offense. If his elder sisters are reputable, his chances are good ; but if they be not reputable, the chances of his becoming an habitual criminal are increased proportionately.

Illegitimacy.—Where harlotry rather than prostitution is common, it is to be expected that the number of illegitimate children will be numerous. Of the 535 children born 335 were legitimate, 106 illegitimate and 84 unknown. Discarding from the computation the 84 who are not ascertained, we get 23.50 per cent as the proportion of illegitimacy, counting both sexes.

TABLE V.

Illegitimacy.

	Boys.	Girls.
Total number of children	224	251
Of legitimate birth	155	190
Of illegitimate birth	49	33
Per cent of bastards to total number, by sex	21.42	13.22
" " " " legitimates, by sex	33.61	17.36
" " " " total number, both sexes		23.50

The above table shows an excess of girls over boys among the legitimate, while there is an excess of boys over girls among the illegitimate, and, when we compare them by percentages, the illegitimate boys are twice as numerous as the girls, 33.61 per cent to 17.36.

If the object of our inquiry rested here, and a generalization upon the above figures were made, based on the conventional and generally accepted effects of illegitimacy on the question of crime and pauperism, the conclusion would be inevitable that the above figures explain the cause of pauperism and crime. The facts being at hand, it is perhaps safer to enter into a more minute inquiry, and pass from the consideration of aggregate numbers, to analyze particular cases.

Of the five " Juke " sisters, three are known to have had illegitimate children, Ada, Bell and Delia.

The two bastards of Delia were lazy ne'er-do-weels, who never married, and are not known to have had children ; but little has been gathered respecting them. Of her legitimate children, one, a girl, was the mother of criminals, and is the only line in the legitimate branches in which crime is found.

Of the children of Ada (see charts I. and II.) the oldest was the father of the distinctively criminal branch of the family. Two of his sons, though never sent to prison, were notorious petty thieves and the fathers of convicted criminals, while two of their daughters were the mothers of criminals. None of the legitimate children or grandchildren of Ada are known to have been criminals.

But while the children and grandchildren of Ada's oldest were criminals, the majority of them were legitimate. Thus we find forty legitimates and five illegitimates among the descendants.

Of the children of Bell (see chart III. generation 3), the first four were illegitimate, three of them mulattoes. The three boys were, on the whole, more successful in life than the average of the "Jukes." They all three acquired property, the youngest being the father of one child who was successful in life, also accumulating property. Of the oldest, a mulatto, a gentleman who knew all the earlier members of the "Juke" stock, says: "He was the best of his generation, being honest, sober, and in every way manly." On the other hand, chart IV., which gives one branch of the posterity of Effie, almost all of whom are legitimate, shows a widespread and almost unbroken record of pauperism.

From these considerations, and others, which are not stated in the review of individual cases because they are only repetitions of cases which are related elsewhere, it follows that illegitimacy is not necessarily the cause of crime and pauperism.

Tentative Inductions.—1. Among the first-born children of lawful marriages, the female sex preponderates.

2. Among the first-born bastard children, the males preponderate.

3. It is not illegitimacy, *per se*, which is dangerous, but the environment of neglect which attends it that is mischievous.

4. Illegitimates who are placed in favorable environment may succeed in life better than legitimate children in the same environment.

Disease and Pauperism.—Running alongside of licentiousness, and as inseparable from it as is illegitimacy, are the diseases which are distinctive of it and which produce social phenomena which are the direct subjects of the present investigation. In the wake of disease follows pauperism, so in studying the one we must necessarily discuss the other. But disease treats of physiological states, it is a biological question ; therefore, the social questions included in the consideration of pauperism rest, in large measure, upon the data furnished by the study of vital force.

Before taking up the statistics of disease, we give those of pauperism to show the general tendency of the family to pauperism, before we study the causes that produce that condition.

Comparing, by sexes, the alms-house relief of the State at large

TABLE VI.

*Of Pauperism, showing Out-door * and Alms-house Relief.*

	Number of persons receiving out-door relief.	Number of years.	Estimated cost at $15 a year.	Number of persons receiving alms-house relief.	Number of years.	Estimated cost at $100 a year.	Total number of persons.	Percentage receiving out-door relief.	Percentage receiving alms-house relief.	Percentage of alms-house pauperism, male, female, and total for New York State in 1871.	Ratio between pauperism of State at large and the Juke family.
Women of the Juke blood..	45	242	$3,630	24	35	$3,500	251	13.94	9.56	1.26	As 1 to 7.590
Men of the Juke blood.....	50	270	4,050	29	46	4,600	224	20.09	12.94	1.39	As 1 to 9.309
Women of the X blood......	20	125	1,875	5	7	700	67	29.85	7.44	1.26	As 1 to 5.900
Men of the X blood........	27	97	1,455	6	8	800	102	26.56	5.88	1.39	As 1 to 4.239
Total number of Juke blood..	95	512	$7,680	53	81	$8,100	540	17.59	9.80	1.33	As 1 to 7.368
Total number of X blood.....	47	222	3,330	11	15	1,500	169	27.81	6.51	1.33	As 1 to 4.893
Grand total.............	142	734	$11,080	64	96	$9,600	709	20.02	9.02	1.33	As 1 to 6.767

* The out-door relief is dispensed by eight poor-masters, who live in four different towns, each town keeping a separate record of names and amounts of help. These records, since the beginning of this century, amount to an aggregate of 225 years, of which only sixty-four years could be consulted, the records of the 191 missing years being in many cases destroyed.

This table exhibits only the amount of relief which this family has obtained as shown by the records.

with that of the " Jukes," we find seven and a half times more pauperism among their women than among the average of women for the State, among their men nine times more, while the average for both sexes of the " Juke " and X blood together gives six and three quarter times more paupers than the average of the State. According to the records of poor-houses and city alms-houses of the State, the men are in excess of the women, the ratio for 1871 being as 100 women is to 110 men ; of the " Jukes " this ratio is as 100 to 124, but when we look at the alms-house relief of the X blood the ratio is inverted, the women being to the men as 100 is to 80. Thus, while the " Jukes " follow the general rule of our State pauperism as respects the comparison of the sexes, the X blood follows a reverse one. Why this is I cannot say, unless it be that the tendency of the women is to follow the condition of their husbands, which involves in the net of pauperism those women marrying into the " Juke " pauper stock, while the " Juke " women, seeking and finding husbands not so involved, are withdrawn from the pauper circle. That this inversion of ratios is not an accident is proved by the fact that the out-door relief of the X blood shows the same relationship, though in a less degree, the ratio being as 100 women are to 90 men.

In table VII. is presented the statistics of diseases, malformations

TABLE VII.

Diseases, Malformations and Injuries.

	Blind.	Deaf and Dumb.	Insane.	Idictic.	Tubercular consumption.	Syphilis.	Constitutional syphilis.	Epilepsy.	Deformed.	Total number injured, deformed and diseased.	Number diseased persons receiving relief.	Percentage.
Juke blood..	10	......	1	1	1	29	22	......	1	65	33	50.77
X blood	1	1	......	......	1	13	3	1	......	20	15	75.00
Total.....	11	1	1	1	2	42	25	1	1	85	48	56.47

and injuries, in their relations to pauperism. In this table children who have died of inherited diseases and were buried by the town, are excluded because they have no significance as causes of pauperism, their early death placing them in the category of effects of disease and pauperism ; nor is any person counted under two headings.

Notice here, while the percentage of pauperism for the whole family is only 22.22 per cent, that of pauperism among the sick and disabled is 56.47 per cent. In one case, the hereditary blindness of one man cost the town twenty-three years of out-door relief for two people and a town burial. Another case of hereditary blindness cost eight years of out-door and three years of poor-house relief, with a town burial.

But the disease which the above table shows as the most common, as incontestably it is the most destructive, subtle and difficult to eradicate, is syphilis. One cause of its great prevalence is that many men deliberately expose themselves to it, because it is accounted a matter of manly prowess to be proof against infection. Their ignorance is such that they count syphilization as indicative of virility. In this exhibit are enumerated only the cases properly vouched for by competent physicians or directly drawn from the records of the poor-house, and six so notorious as to be trustworthy. Here, the proportion of those blighted by it reaches 10.86 per cent, but this does not include half of the victims of this class of disorders. On the authority of physicians who know, from twenty-five to thirty per cent are tainted with it. Significant as are these aggregate figures, they are weak as compared to the lesson which is pointed when we analyze the lines along which this disease runs, and note its devastation of individual careers and its pauperizing influence on successive generations. If it were merely the record of so many human beings who have simply died, it would lose most of its significance ; but in view that this is the record of so many who have lived maimed lives, maimed in numberless ways ; entailing maimed lives full of weakness, which is wretchedness ; sapping the vitality of innocent ones to the third and fourth generations in a constantly broadening stream, and breeding complex social disorders growing out of these physiological degenerations, the question

grows into larger and more momentous proportions the more mi-
nutely we look into it.

In chart II. the following five cases in consanguineous stock
can be traced and compared.

Case 7. Line 1, generation 3, (2) l. m. A., the progenitor, was
a volunteer in 1812, a very licentious man, who contracted malignant syphilis in the army before his marriage to his cousin.
This disease he entailed upon his eight children, seven of them
girls, and the combined effects of it and the consanguinity of the
parentage have produced marked social effects. He was twice an
inmate of the same alms-house, at 45 and at 52.

Case 8. Line 24, generation 4, was his daughter, a congenital
idiot. At eight she drifted into the poor-house and remained there
eight years. Whether she was removed or died the imperfect
records do not show : she is probably dead. Here the correlation
between the physical and social condition is established. It is a case
of absolute hereditary pauperism, the entailment depending on disease in one generation producing cerebral atrophy in the next ; for
idiocy has been described as " arrest of development," * chiefly of
the brain and of the nervous system, proceeding from insufficient
nutrition during ante-natal life, and brought about by diverse causes,
the most frequent of which is scrofulous or syphilitic disease in the
parents. Pauperism here stands as the social equivalent of disease,
which is a form of weakness.

Case 9. Line 3, generation 5, is another case of alms-house
pauperism two removes from the grandfather, whose licentiousness
is the original cause of this condition. This girl's mother, an elder
sister of the above idiot, is tainted so deeply with constitutional
syphilis that she is weak-minded and blind. Six out of eight of
her children died young, and the vitality of the two surviving girls
was impaired. Here, inheritable disease precedes, pauperism
follows, a generation having been skipped, that overleaped generation itself surely gravitating to the poor-house. Tracing the environment we find the example of licentiousness in each generation,—

---

* Idiocy, etc., Edward Seguin, N. Y., 1866, pp. 40, 41.

the grandfather, the mother who keeps a brothel and the daughter who is sent to the poor-house as "a vagrant," an official euphonism for prostitute. Here the environment runs parallel to the heredity and is contributive to the perpetuation of the specific disease, causing the blighted granddaughter to revert to the social condition of the grandfather, pauperism.

Case 10. Line 13, generation 6, has been given before in case 2, when considering harlotry; we now examine it as a question of pauperism. She is a great granddaughter of the progenitor, an infant mulatto girl conceived by the roadside, born in a poor-house and killed by syphilis before her first year. Thus the granddaughter's licentiousness prepares for her child the identical fate which her grandfather's debauchery did for his idiotic daughter (case 7), premature death linked to alms-house life. Going back along the same line to generation 4, we find other forms of disease linked to pauperism. The mother, affected with constitutional syphilis, is married first to a "Juke" husband who dies at forty in the poor-house, of consumption. For at least three years before his death (the records previous to this time are missing) she, at thirty-one, and her husband, at thirty-eight, received out-door relief. The second husband also dies of consumption, but in some other town, so that it has been impossible to get the poor-master's record. Of this generation three of the Jukes find a home in the alms-house. Tracing back to the third generation, we find the syphilitic father at forty-five, in the same place, and again later at fifty-two. The year and cause of his death have not been ascertained, so this example is incomplete, but these preliminary conclusions may be educed: Disease in the third, fourth and sixth generations, and youth in the fourth, both of them forms of weakness, produce a social equivalent, pauperism.

Case 11. Line 18 is an illegitimate girl twelve years old, her mother being a prostitute with a constitution broken by syphilis. Eleven years ago she died at about 39, and the child was sent to the poor-house. From thence she was adopted by a lady of wealth and is looked upon by some of her relations as having a brilliant future. Here again we find disease bringing with it premature

2*   C

death to the mother, pauperism to the child. It is a case of weakness, its form youth.

So far only instances of hereditary pauperism produced by disease have been set forth, we now examine cases of induced pauperism proceeding from different causes.

Case 12. Taking chart I. (1), b. m. A., generation 3, and passing to the first child of the next generation, we find a man whose wife died of syphilis when he was fifty-three. At that age he had become an habitual drunkard, and although a good workman, became idle. He obtained out-door relief during her sickness, and for twenty years since has been a charge upon the town, but he has never been in the poor-house. On the mother's death the fourth child aged fourteen, the fifth aged twelve, the sixth aged eight, the seventh aged seven, the eighth aged four, and the ninth child aged two years were sent to the poor-house, and there remained four years. Two years after her death, the third child goes to the poor-house at seventeen, and is immediately bound out to a farmer, while the two eldest, being respectively twenty-four and twenty-nine, are not sent. Here again we find youth, which is weakness, consigns the child to the influence of the poor-house, while the elder escape it by reason of their strength. Here disease produces induced pauperism of the father and in the offspring. It is an instance of the tendency of the youngest child to be the pauper of the family, which will be discussed further on.

Case 13. The second child (l. f., A. B.), a girl, seems to be an exception to the rule laid down, for we find her, seven years before her mother's death, and at the age of eighteen, one month in the poor-house, to bring her first born, an illegitimate boy, into the world. Here the maternal functions produces temporary weakness, which is the essential of pauperism.

Case 14. This is similar in some aspects to case 11. In chart II., generation 3, (4) l. f. A., we find a legitimate daughter who marries a mulatto X. For some reason which has not been learned, the father ceases to maintain his family. The mother, near her confinement, with no relations to volunteer the expense of her sickness, becomes an inmate of the poor-house, with the three youngest children, at which place the fourth child is born. Comparing the children of the fourth generation, we find the older ones escape the influence of the poor-house at this time, no doubt because their strength enables them to support themselves. Here again we find weakness makes the pauper, the children because of youth, the mother because of inability to earn bread for a large family.

Cases 12 and 14 illustrate that the tendency of the youngest child is to become the pauper of the family and furnish data which help to explain why it is so. The child who is born in the poor-house, especially if a girl, stands a very fair chance of remaining there till 10 or 14 years of age, before anybody thinks it worth while to adopt her. She has then formed an affection for the place, its people, and its habits, and when the vicissitudes of life bring want, she fails in effort, the traditions of youth having prepared her to rely on help, she reverts easily to the poor-house even in the prime of life. The older children, not having any such experience, are less likely to think of it as an alternative.

We now take up a different class of cases which show that the tendency of the youngest is to be the pauper of the family, adding another form of proof to establish that proposition.

Case 15. Chart I., children of the eldest born of generation 3 compared to each other. The first born in generation 4 begins his claim for outside relief at 53, his next brother at 36, and the youngest born boy at 46, indicating a power of resistance greater in the first born than in the last. The only child of this generation who enters the poor-house is a girl, and she is the youngest child, who gets committed for debauchery.

That the youngest boy resists better than the third is owing, probably, to his having married a wife who was healthy and whose industrious habits checked the tendency to induced pauperism, while the wife of the eldest brother being fat and syphilitic, becomes a burden upon him by reason of disease, conditions contributive to discouragement of domestic affections and to the exertion for the maintenance of home which those motives arouse.

Case 16. Passing to chart III., and comparing the eight children of Bell, the first four of whom are illegitimate, we find the fourth and the eighth child are inclined to pauperism. This seems to contradict the rule that the youngest is the pauper of the family ; but we must take into consideration that the fifth child is the son of a legitimate marriage, and may probably be the first child of his father, so that the continuity of the line is broken and gives us two sets of examples in the children of the same mother. The eldest children of each set are self-supporting and independent, the illegitimates being the most so.

Now, comparing the age at which the out-door relief begins, we find the fourth child applies at 66, three years before his death, when he receives a town burial, while the youngest applies at 55, and receives outside relief for 23 years, when his career closes with a town burial. The fourth son acquired a farm of 60 acres, was industrious but rough, and intemperate in his older days. His farm was lost, and he died prematurely. The eighth son never acquired property, was temperate, but blind for many years with cataract and died of old age.

In both these cases we find forms of weakness, intemperance and blindness, both physiological conditions predisposing to pauperism, but there is no alms-house relief.

Case 17. Passing to the children of the fourth child of Bell (gen. 4, lines 4 to 14) we find the oldest son (line 4) independent, industrious and prosperous. The second (line 5) receives out-door relief from 65 to his death, the sixth (line 13) getting it at 38, and the seventh, a girl, at 30, entering the poor-house at 40 with her two children.

Here the same tendency is to be found as in other cases indicated.

Case 18. Now we turn to chart IV., analyzing the progeny of Effie, a line distinctively pauperized. In the third generation we have traced only two persons, a son and daughter. The son, in his 87th year, entered the poor-house and died there in 1859, aged 90. The daughter married into X, who, at the age of 40, became an inmate of the poor-house for a short time. The next account we have of him is that at 80 he was again in the poor-house, where he died the following year ; the record of out-door relief which he received being among the years which could not be obtained.

Taking the next generation of this daughter, and comparing

her male children, we find the first boy, aged 64, gets out-door relief at 30, the second at 22, the third at 24, the fifth at 24. If we take the age of entering the poor-house, we get first child, 56 ; second, 47 ; third, 23 ; fourth, 42 ; the discrepancies are owing partly to the records being imperfect and to the better character of the wives.

Line 1, generation 5, chart IV., presents an exception to the general rule, the man in this case being the eldest of the family. The consideration of this is postponed till we enter on the relation of pauperism to crime, for this seeming exception brings into relief other relations which can be best appreciated when we have discussed and examined further.

Case 19. In chart IV., taking lines 8 to 13 inclusive, we find in generation 5 six children in the poor-house ; going back to the next generation, father in poor-house ; going back to generation 3, again we find the poor-house. Such is the heredity.

The environment of the fifth generation at the time they entered the poor-house was that the father was serving a term in the county jail for breach of peace ; the support of the family was gone, with the result noted. The environment beyond this is not known.

The administration of the poor laws in this county must be taken into consideration in weighing the environment. For at least three generations the giving of out-door relief has been used by the poor-masters as a means of winning and retaining the votes of that portion of the population who would avail themselves of it, thus adding a powerful incentive to increase induced pauperism, political aspirants thrusting public charity upon many who would otherwise have been ashamed to ask for it.

Tentative Inductions on Pauperism.—In summing up this branch of the inquiry the following preliminary inductions may be stated as the laws of pauperism which are applicable to the case in hand, and may upon a broader basis of facts prove to be general laws applicable to pauperism in general :

1. Pauperism is an indication of weakness of some kind, either youth, disease, old age, injury ; or, for women, childbirth.

2. It is divisible into hereditary and induced pauperism.

3. Hereditary pauperism rests chiefly upon disease in some form, tends to terminate in extinction, and may be called the sociological aspect of physical degeneration.

4. The debility and diseases which enter most largely in its production are the result of sexual licentiousness.

5. Pauperism in adult age, especially in the meridian of life, indicates a hereditary tendency which may or may not be modified by the environment.

6. Pauperism follows men more frequently than women, indicating a decided tendency to hereditary pauperism.

7. The different degrees of adult pauperism from out-door relief to alms-house charity, indicate, in the main, different gradations of waning vitality. In this light the whole question is opened up, whether indolence, which the dogmatic aphorism says "is the root of all evil," is not, after all, a mark of undervitalization and an effect which acts only as a secondary cause.

8. Induced pauperism results from bad administration of the law, or temporary weakness or disability in the recipient.

9. The pauperism of childhood is an accident of life rather than a hereditary characteristic.

10. The youngest child has a tendency to become the pauper of the family.

11. Youngest children are more likely than the older ones to become the inmates of the poor-house through the misconduct or misfortune of parents.

12. Such younger children, who remain inmates of the alms-house long enough to form associations that live in the memory and habits that continue in the conduct, have a greater tendency to spontaneously revert to that condition whenever any emergency of life overtakes them, and domesticate there more readily than older children whose greater strength has kept them out during youth.

13. The children old enough to provide for themselves are forced by necessity to rely upon themselves, and in consequence are less liable to become paupers in old age.

14. Induced pauperism may lead to the establishment of the hereditary form.

In consideration of the last three propositions, which relate to environment, and show how great an influence it has on determining the career, is added a further proposition, which is dogmatically put forth, though not fully sustained by the facts enumerated in the present study.

15. Pauperism, which depends on social and educational disabilities and not upon deep-seated constitutional disease, can and must be prevented by sound and felicitous measures of administration that will conform to modes of dealing with it spontaneously adopted by society and are therefore as generally acceptable as they will prove efficacious.

Intemperance.—Certain considerations have made me hesitate to accept the current opinions as to the part which ardent spirits play in the carnival of crime. The temperance agitation has for many years taken a partisan character and become an "element of politics," with this inevitable result, that the discussion of the subject has been shifted from the domain of dispassionate observation into that of sentimental agitation, the conclusions arrived at being of the nature of hasty deductions from cherished opinions, and equally hasty or equally erroneous inductions from irrelevant facts.

It is remembered that the value of the present inquiry rests on the method of viewing the course of generations chronologically and of recording the facts of each life in the order of their occurrence. In conformity with this some of the prominent points that need special observation in the study of intemperance seem to be, when was drinking first begun ; when was habitual intemperance fixed ; what were the sexual habits at various periods, especially in youth ; whether any deep-seated disease has preceded or followed the intemperate habits, what kind, and whether causing it or not; whether excessive study or labor has exhausted the vitality ; whether there is a hereditary predisposition ; whether the trade or occupation is detrimental to health ; whether the locality of the habitation produces disease, and what kind ; what is the temperament of the man? All these questions must be answered by ascertained facts before we can give an intelligent answer to the question, " Is intemperance the cause of crime and pauperism ? " or only a secondary cause that must be reached by well-ordered sanitary, hygienic and educational measures. The following table gives a statement of facts, taking care not to draw rash conclusions, most of those who are marked healthy are not licentious. Of the three who were licentious before intemperance, the following particulars :

TABLE VIII.

Comparing temperance and intemperance.

	Healthy.	Diseased.	Licentious.	Chaste.	Licentious previous to intemperate.	Diseased previous to.	Total.
Temperate.....................	18	1	7	....	....	....	26
Intemperate	3	10	29	....	....	3	45

Case 20. Take chart III., generation 3, line 4, and we have (4) b. m. B. He was industrious in early life, accumulated property, was of a tough, coarse-grained temperament, and in his youth licentious. He is not known ever to have been a criminal, but he did become a drunkard in middle life, lost his property, and died of premature old age, at 69 receiving a town burial.

In this case we find licentiousness in youth, drunkenness when the meridian of life is passed, premature death.

Case 21. Chart I., line 41, generation 5, we have a man, m. X, who was licentious in his youth, who had contracted syphilis, and who, on the decline of life, was a sot, and hastened his death by his excesses in drink. The same general course as the last case, licentiousness, intemperance, premature death.

Case 22. Chart I., line 27, generation 5, a woman (5), l. f. A. B. X, who began prostitution at an early age ; at 25 was a drunkard. She then joined the church ; shortly after, she married and left off her licentious habits. She is now reported as being less given to drunkenness then she was ten years ago.

The law faintly shadowed forth by this scanty evidence is that licentiousness has preceded the use of ardent spirits and probably caused a physical exhaustion that made stimulants grateful. Additional evidence as to the view here put forth will be found on page 93, where hereditary and other phenomena are tabulated. This fuller investigation tends to show that certain diseases and mental disorders precede the appetite for stimulants, and that the true cause of their use is the antecedent hereditary or induced physical exhaustion ; the remedy, healthy, well-balanced constitutions. If this view should prove correct, one of the great points in the training of paupers and criminal children will be to pay special attention to sexual training, and to prevent and cure constitutional diseases which may have come to them as a heritage. It also shows that the intemperance question is one for the physician and educator to deal with rather than the legislator.

Crime.—In the table here appended, as only official records of crimes are entered, two principal causes for the smallness of the number of offenses need explaining. As respects crimes, the records of only one county were examined, and these reached back only to 1830; the earlier records. your committee was told, are down in the cellar of the county clerk's office, under the coal. To get a full record of the crimes of the " Juke " family the criminal records of three other counties need to be examined. As respects misdemeanors, these are to be found in the books of justices of the peace and the books of the sheriffs, both of which are either destroyed or laid away in private hands, packed in barrels or stowed in garrets, and are inaccessible. In addition we must note that in the latter part of the last century and the beginning of this, many acts which now subject a man to imprisonment then went unpunished, even cases of murder, arson and highway robbery, so that the absence of a man's name from the criminal calendar is no criterion of his honesty.

In the first place, the illegitimates who have become parent stocks are the oldest children of their respective mothers, Ada, Bell and Delia ; but as the bastards of the latter had no children, this leaves only those of her other sisters to be considered. In the study of crime we take the males as the leading sex, skipping the women just as in studying harlotry we skipped the men, but at the same time it will be well to notice how harlotry prevails among those families where the boys are criminals.

Case 23. Take chart I., generation 3, line 1, we get an intermarriage of cousins, and the appearance of crime seems to be postponed for a generation. The word " seems " is used because no crime receiving punishment was committed ; but there is no doubt that the two eldest sons of the next generation were both petty thieves, one of them an expert sheep stealer. Coming down to the next generation (5th) we find the criminal children to be where there is a cross between the " Juke " and the X blood. We also find that the oldest male child of the fourth generation is the father of proportionately more criminals than the second male child, while the third male child, who is also the youngest and has intermarried into the " Juke " blood, is the father of honest children. The figures run thus : 1st son, 7 boys, 5 criminals ; 2d son, 6 boys, 2 criminals ; 3d son, 4 boys, no criminals.

Moreover, comparing the children of the fifth generation by families, we find that it is the older brothers who are the criminals and not the younger ones ; while, if we trace down line 1 to the 6th generation, we find the heredity of crime seems to run in the line of the oldest child, and that the males preponderate in those lines.

Case 24. Taking the illegitimate progeny of Bell, chart III., what do we find : that the preponderance is of males, and that the three eldest children are honest, industrious and self-supporting.

The probable reason for the honesty of the first born children will be discussed further on. But when we come to the fourth child we find, what ? That he has married outside the " Juke" blood ; that he is not a criminal himself, but that amongst his children are found criminals. The oldest of his boys, as in the previous generation, was industrious. He married, emigrated to Pennsylvania at least 30 years ago, and now owns a farm and is doing well.

The second child was a farmer and industrious, lived to 70 years of age, and neither committed crime nor went to the county-house, but received out-door relief at 65 for 3 years. The third child did tolerably well and had no criminal children, they being all girls.

TABLE IX.

CRIMES AGAINST PROPERTY.

		NUMBER OF OFFENSES.												
		2d Gen.		3d Gen.		4th Gen.		5th Gen.		6th Gen.		Total.		Total.
		M.	F.	M.	F.	M.	F.	M.	F.	M.	F.	M.	F.	
Misdemeanor	Juke..	..	..	1	..	7	6	14	14	1	2	24	22	..
	X ...	..	..	1	..	1	1	8	1	..	..	9	3	..
Petit larceny	Juke..	..	..	..	..	1	..	6	..	..	..	7	..	..
	X	..	..	..	..	3	..	2	..	..	..	5	.	..
Grand larceny	Juke	..	..	..	..	..	..	..	..	..	..	..	..	..
	X	..	..	..	..	1	..	2	..	..	..	3	..	..
Burglary	Juke..	..	..	..	..	2	..	11	..	..	..	..	..	..
	X	..	..	..	..	2	1	..	..	..	..	..	..	..
Forgery	Juke..	..	..	..	..	..	..	..	..	..	..	1	..	.
	X	..	..	..	..	1	..	..	..	..	..	1	..	..
False pretenses	Juke..	..	..	..	..	..	..	..	..	..	..	1	..	..
	X	..	..	1	..	..	..	..	..	..	..	1	..	..
Robbery	Juke..	..	..	..	..	..	..	1	..	..	..	1	..	..
	X	..	..	..	..	..	..	..	..	..	..	..	..	..
Total	Juke..	..	..	1	..	10	6	32	14	1	2	44	22	66
	X	..	..	2	..	8	2	12	1	.		22	3	25
Grand total, offenses		..	..	3	..	18	8	44	15	1	2	66	25	91
Number of offenders.	Juke..	..	..	1	..	8	4	12	9	1	2	22	15	37
	X	2	..	2	..	6	2	8	1	..	..	16	3	19
Total		2	..	3	..	14	6	20	10	1	2	38	18	56

CRIMES AGAINST THE PERSON.

		M.	F.	M.	F.	M.	F.	M.	F.	M.	F.	M.	F.	
Assault and battery	Juke..	..	..	..	..	3	..	3	..	..	..	6	..	..
	X	..	..	..	..	1	..	3	..	..	..	4	..	..
Assault, intent to kill	Juke..	..	..	..	..	1	1	..	..	1	..	2	1	..
	X	..	..	..	..	..	..	..	..	..	..	..	..	..
Murder	Juke..	..	..	..	..	1	..	1	..	..	..	2	..	..
	X	1	..	..	..	2	..	1	..	..	..	4	..	..
Rape, and attempt at rape.	Juke..	..	..	..	..	..	..	5	..	..	..	5	..	..
	X	..	..	..	..	..	..	..	..	..	..	..	..	..
Total offenses	Juke..	..	..	..	..	5	1	9	..	1	..	15	1	16
	X	1	..	..	..	3	..	4	..	..	..	8	..	8
Grand total, offenses		1	..	..	..	8	1	13	..	1	..	23	1	24
Number of offenders.	Juke..	..	..	..	..	4	1	6	..	1	..	11	1	12
	X	1	..	..	..	4	..	4	..	..	..	9	..	9
Total number of offenders....		1	..	..	..	8	1	10	..	1	..	20	1	21

The fourth was a criminal and died of syphilitic consumption ; the fifth was the father of a criminal ; also the sixth, who had received outside relief at 38 years of age; while the seventh, and last, was a harlot and an alms-house pauper, who died of syphilitic disease.

Here we see crime immediately follows the cross of bloods, and that the criminal is born before the pauper of the family, as we also see that the honest is born before the criminal. It now remains to follow several lines, tracing the heredity of individual cases, and laying the environment alongside.

Case 25. Chart I., line 1, generation 6, gives a boy 17 years of age, who has served six months in Albany penitentiary for petit larceny; his father (gen. 5th) has been twice in county jail for assault and battery, and is now serving a five-year sentence in State prison for a rape on his niece in her twelfth year. Going further back we find the father was a petty thief, though never convicted. This ends the information as to the heredity. Now as to the environment.

The adults of generation 4 lived in a settlement mainly composed of their own relatives, situated in the woods around a chain of lakes. The great proportion of these people having recourse to petty theft to help out their uncertain incomes, going on excursions of several miles during the night, and robbing hen-roosts, stripping clothes-lines, breaking into smoke-houses and stealing hams, corn, firewood and wood with which to make axe-handles, baskets or chair-bottoms This general condition continued during the boyhood of generation 5, only, the general wealth of the community having enormously increased their field became broader and their offenses more grave than those of the previous generation. Going down to generation 6, we find the boy of 17 is suddenly deprived of support by his father being sent to prison. He is in want; his mother goes to the poor-house with the younger children, while he takes up the life of a vagrant, picking up his living as he best can. Want, bad company, neglect form the environment that predisposes to larceny. He will not go to the county-house with his mother; he feels it is more independent to steal and takes the risks. Now self-reliance, no matter how wrongly it asserts itself, is indicative of power, and this power should be availed of for better purposes. In these three generations is traced an environment which predisposes to crime and corresponds to the heredity.

Case 26. Now turning to line 4 of the sixth generation, a boy 19 years of age throws another boy over a cliff forty feet high, out of malicious mischief. This boy is the second illegitimate child of his mother, but probably not of his father, which latter was the first illegitimate child of his mother by X. This case then seems to follow the rule that the crime follows the lines of illegitimacy where the "Juke" blood marries into X. There is no evidence that the mother was a criminal, but her father was a petty thief, as shown by chart I. Such is the heredity.

The environment, a home the scene of violence, debauch and drunkenness, father and mother both intemperate and idle; the mother becoming the procuress for her eldest son of a child 12 years of age, whom that illegitimate son seduces and is forced to marry to prevent criminal prosecution; the first born of this child forming the third bastard in a line of heredity. Here we have an environment corresponding to the heredity.

Case 27. Line 22, generation 5, seems to be an exception to the rule that the oldest is a criminal, but it is only a seeming exception. He, with his next brother aged 12, engaged in a burglary, getting $100 in gold as booty. The boy was caught, but he, the leader in the crime, escaped. Being a sailor, it is impossible to get any reliable information about his career, but it is evident that at 19 he was a leader in crime.

Case 28. Of lines 33, 34 and 37 in the fifth generation, brothers and sisters, we find the oldest son commits a number of offenses, among them murder, but he escapes punishment as in the case above. The second child, a girl, has become the contriver of the crimes which the third child, a boy, has carried into effect, and for which he has recently received 20 years' sentence of imprisonment. In this case the boldest and most intelligent is the oldest child.

Of the crimes committed by the legitimate branch of the Juke family no chart has been made, only that the same general rule holds good, that the eldest is the criminal of the family, the youngest the pauper.

TABLE X.

Showing the Contrast between the Distinctively Pauper and the Distinctively Criminal Branches.

	Total number of males.	No. receiving it.	OUT-DOOR RELIEF — Per cent.	No. of years.	No. of years for each person.	Age of youngest adult receiving.	No. under 20 years who receive it.	No. over 35 years and under 40 who first received.	No. over 45 who first receive it.	No. receiving it.	ALMS-HOUSE RELIEF — Per cent.	No. of years.	No. of years to each person.	Children under 15 receiving it.	Age of youngest adult receiving it.	No. of adults under 30 receiving it.	No. of adults over 35 receiving it.	No. of adults over 50 receiving it.
Juke males (I) A. ᴹ B. branch	28	10	35.71	48	4.80	19	1	4	2	6	21.42	17	2.833	5	17	1		
Juke males E. ᴹ X. branch	13	8	61.54	52	6.50	17	3			5	38.86	5	1.000	1	23	1	2	1
Criminal males (I) A. ᴹ B.	17	6	35.30	38	6.333	*19	8	2	3	4	23.53	9	2.250	8	17	1		
Criminal males E. ᴹ X.	7	7	100.00	44	6.285	17	1			4	57.14	4	1.000		23	1	2	1

* Town burial.

TABLE X.—(Continued).

	No. of criminals.	Per cent to total males.	No. of offenses.	No. of offenses to each criminal.	Offenses agt. property.	Per ct to total offenses.	Offenses against the person.	Per ct to total offenses.	Vagrancy, breach of peace.	Percentage to total offenses.	Years of prison or penitentiary.	Average No. of years to each person.	Years of county jail.	AGAINST PROPERTY — Highest crime.	Lowest crime.	AGAINST PERSON — Highest crime.	Lowest crime.	Longest sentence, years.
Juke males (I) A. ᴹ B. branch	17	60.71	42	2.470	23	54.76	12	28.57	7	16.68	70¾	1.132	1¼	Burglary, 1st. H. robbery.. Petit larceny.	.... Petit larceny.	Murder. Rape... Attempt to kill.	Assault and battery.	30 5
Juke males E. ᴹ branch	7	53.84	13	1.857	4	30.77	4	30.77	6	46.15	5	.7143	¾				Assault and battery.	

Tentative Inductions respecting Crime :

1. The burden of crime is found in the illegitimate lines.

2. The legitimate lines marry into crime.

3. Those streaks of crime found in the legitimate lines are found chiefly where there have been crosses into X.

4. The eldest child has a tendency to be the criminal of the family.

5. Crime chiefly follows the male lines.

6. The longest lines of crime are along the line of the eldest son.

Crime and Pauperism compared.—The ideal pauper is the idiotic adult unable to help himself, who may be justly called a living embodiment of death. The ideal criminal is a courageous man in the prime of life who so skilfully contrives crime on a large scale that he escapes detection and succeeds in making the community believe him to be honest as he is generous. Between these two extremes there are endless gradations which approximate each other, till at last you reach a class who are too weak to be contrivers of crime, and too strong to be alms-house paupers ; they are the tools who execute what others plan and constitute the majority of those who are found in prison during their youth and prime, and in the poor-house in their old age. These men prefer the risks and excitements of criminality and the occasional confinement of a prison where they meet congenial company, to the security against want and the stagnant life of the alms-house.

To more fully illustrate this we give table X., in which is made a comparison of the distinctively criminal branch of Ada, with the distinctively pauper branch of Effie, so that the difference can be contrasted. It will be seen that while the criminal branch shows 35 per cent of out-door relief and 21 per cent of alms-house paupers, with 60 per cent of crime, the pauper branch shows 61 per cent of out-door relief, 38 per cent of, alms-house pauperism, and 53 per cent of crime. But when we come to study the intensity of crime, we find that while nine offenders of the line of Ada have been sent to State prison for 60 years, only one has been sent for five years or the line of Effie. Again, contrasting the crimes against property, against person and vagrancy, the percentages show great disparities. While Ada's offspring perpetrate 54 per cent of crimes against property, including burglary, grand larceny, and highway robbery, Effie's only show 30 per cent, the highest crime being petit larceny, which is the lowest crime of the other branch. Of the crimes against the person, Effie's stock shows a preponderance, 30 per cent, compared to 28 per cent, while the offenses compare as to intensity: Effie's, attempt to kill, one; Ada's, murder one, attempt at rape, three. When we come to breach of peace and vagrancy the percentage stands between Ada's and Effie's children as 16 to 46 per cent, and for vagrancy as 2 to 38 per cent. Comparing the criminals of each branch to each other, we find while all of Effie's are pauperized, only 35 per cent of Ada's have received out-door relief, while the alms-house pauperism compare as 23 per cent of Ada, to 57 per cent of Effie. Looking still closer and comparing ages at which relief was received, we find only one of Ada to five of Effie received out-door relief under 25 years of age, while two of Ada's resisted application till after 35, and one after 45, while every one of Effie's seven criminals was a pauper before 35—in point of fact at 30. The contrast as to the alms-house pauperism appears in the table much less than it really is, for, while Ada's account has three children in the poor-house whose ages range from four to ten, Effie's are all adults, ranging from 23 to 56 years of age.

From this comparison, it would seem that the distinctively pauper stock is less aggressive than the criminal, that crimes of contrivance are characteristic of the criminal branch, while petty misdemeanors are the characteristic of the pauper criminal.

Case 29. Having summed up the evidence on pauperism and crime, we now turn to chart IV., generation 5, line 1, to a man who forms an example of the transition state between the two. He is the illegitimate first son of a first son; what his early childhood was has not been ascertained beyond this, that he was not an inmate of an alms-house. His youth was licentious, for at 13 he was afflicted so severely with syphilis, that his foot was lamed for life, and at 41, the time when he was seen, he walked with a halting step. The records show that at 23 years of age he got out-door relief; at 25, petit larceny, county jail; at 30, petit larceny, no one prosecutes; 32, out-door relief one year; 33, prosecuted for bastardy. He compounded this suit by marrying the girl ; at 38, out-door relief ; at 41, petit larceny, county jail 30 days ; assault and battery when drunk, county jail 20 days. This year I saw him at the house of the poor-master, making application for an axe to do wood-chopping, bringing a friend along to ask for a pair of boots. The axe played the ostensible part of honest intentions to work, so that the boots might be forthcoming. Both were denied, and justly. Apparently he realizes in his own person the prepotency of a first child and the weakness of an invalid, as if it might be a conflict between vitality and death, but the side upon which the balance must ultimately fall was decided at 13. He cannot escape being an alms-house pauper except by the interposition of sudden death, because the disability under which he labors is a deep-seated disease, which year by year with cumulative force adds to his inefficiency. Although the eldest child of his generation, he has received out-door relief at an earlier age than his brothers, his disease standing as the equivalent of weakness, and inducing an apathy which destroys both physical activity and pride.

Tentative Inductions on the Relations of Crime and Pauperism :

1. Crime as compared to pauperism indicates vigor.

2. With true criminals pauperism either occurs in old age or in childhood, and is not synchronous with the term of the crime career.

3. Imprisonment of the parent may produce induced pauperism in the children, especially if they be girls who are thrown into the alms-house and remain inmates long enough to become mothers.

4. Criminal careers are more easily modified by environment, because crime, more especially contrived crime, is an index of capacity, and wherever capacity is found, there environment is most effective in producing modifications of career.

5. The misfortune of one generation which throws the children into an alms-house, may lay the foundation for a criminal career for that generation if the children are of an enterprising temperament, for paupers if of low vitality and early licentious habits.

3   D

6. Where an adult oscillates between the poor-house and the jail, it raises a presumption there is either acquired disease or an entailment of bodily or mental weakness from the parents.

7. What is called the deterrent effect of punishment may be only a hastening of the assumption of the pauper condition by such under-vitalized adults. It marks a phase in the effort to gain a living in the direction of least resistance.

8. The tendency of pauperized criminals is to commit misdemeanors or crimes against person.

9. Hereditary pauperism seems to be more fixed than hereditary crime, for very much of crime is the misdirection of faculty and is amenable to discipline, while very much of pauperism is due to the absence of vital power, the lines of pauperism being in many cases identical with such lines of organic disease of mind or body as insanity, consumption, syphilis, which cause from generation to generation, the successive extinction of capacity till death supervenes.

10. Rape, especially of little girls, is a crime of weakness, and, when occurring after the meridian of life has passed (from 35 to 45), marks the decadence of vitality and the consequent weakening of the will-power over the passions.

Relations of Honesty, Crime and Pauperism.—It has already been noticed that the illegitimate children of Bell were industrious and honest, and that the eldest, a mulatto, was " the best of his generation," while the fourth child was the father of criminals. On following down to the next generation of this fourth child, we find the two eldest children honest, the first one acquiring property, the fourth one a criminal contriving crime, and the two next children the parents of criminals, while the youngest is a pauper. In the most vigorous branches honesty and industry are first in order, crime second, and pauperism third. This order may be observed in the following cases :

Case 30. In Bell's stock, chart III. (lines 1 to 15), children, grandchildren, and great-grandchildren.

Third Generation. { 1st. Honesty and industry, with honest descendants.
2d. Honesty and industry, with descendants honest, criminal and pauper, in the order named.

Fourth Generation.
{
1st. Honesty, industry and worldly success.
2d. Honesty and indusrty without worldly success.
3d. Personally criminal.
4th. Non-criminal, but father of criminals.
5th. Non-criminal, pauperized.
}

Case 31. Now look at chart I. children of Ada's illegitimate stock (lines 1 to 13) :

Fifth Generation.
{
1. Criminal and father of criminals.
2. Criminal and not father of criminals, reform with resumption of honest labor.
3. Non-criminal, but inefficient.
4. Pauperized.
}

Taking the third child of generation 4 and analyzing the progeny, lines 22 to 32 :

Fifth Generation.
{
1. Criminal.
2. Criminal, reformed.
3. Non-criminal.
4. Pauperized.
}

Here the same general tendency is noted in the comparison of the children of the same generation. In the discussion of the features of crime we found the tendency to hereditary crime to be along the line of the eldest male child : there is probability that the same is true of the tendency to hereditary honesty, although I have at present no facts to establish it. Descending from the comparison of families to the analysis of individual careers, we get the same essential facts in a different form, and in a way that brings us to a comprehension of some of the underlying causes of them.

Case 32. Take l. m. A. B. X., chart I., generation 5, line 1. At 30 years of age he commits grand larceny, and is sent to the county jail for ninety days. From that time he gets committed no more till he is 49, when he is sent to Sing Sing five years for rape of his niece, 12 years old. In other words, during the prime of life, when the judgment and the will have most control over the emotions, the man's tendency is to give up crime and live by industry. But after he passes his prime we find him committing a crime of weakness, and it will repay to study it carefully.

The order in which the cerebral functions are developed are : 1st. The nervous centres of reflex action ; 2d. The sensations ; 3d. The passions and emotions ; 4th. The judgment and the will, which reach their maximum power from 28 to 33 years of age. The order of their decay is substantially in an inverse progression. Upon looking over the statistics of the crime of rape I find that, for the young, the age of maximum passion is 27, before the full development of the judgment and will ; that the fewest occur between the ages of 32 and 35, the age of maximum will-power ; but from this time we get again an increase in the percentage of this offense. And why ? Because the will, which is the moral governor, tends to decay sooner than the erotic passions, and the man's mind has lost, in part, the moral balance which it possessed at 35, hence opportunity then becomes temptation. This disposes in a general way of the main features of the phenomena of the growth and decay of the organic life, but in this case there is a still further lesson in the study of the environment which was contributive to the act. The circumstances which determined this particular offense accord with the theory of action taking the direction of least resistance. His niece accompanied him alone to go fishing ; now fishing is not an employment requiring labor of either mind or body, and so we find *the* element conspiring to produce the crime is idleness, which left the full vitality of the man to wreak itself in the direction of licentiousness. Laying aside the collateral lesson here, and returning to the main fact to be noted in the chain of argument, the features of it correspond to the essential phenomena of growth, that, being punished for an offense at 30 just before the meridian of life, his career is amended during that period, but, as age approaches with its attendant weakness, he breaks out at 49 into another form of crime, consonant with the decline of life.

Case 33. Take line 7, generation 5, brother of the above. At 22 he was a boatman, and in company with his brother-in-law he commits a burglary, third degree, for which he serves sentence of three years in Sing Sing. Discharged at 25 years of age, he ceases crime and becomes an honest laborer, abandons boating on canal, which is a vagrant occupation, and settles down. He is now described by his employer as a steady, civil and reliable man. The three years' continuous labor in prison, together with the fulness of development attending maturity, have produced steady habits. Here he gets industrial training before the meridian of life, and his career is measurably amended.

Case 34. The next brother, line 8, begins his career with petit larceny at 12, 60 days in county jail ; petit larceny again at 21, county jail 30 days ; grand larceny at 21, Sing Sing 3 years. The probabilities are that between 12 and 21 he committed offenses elsewhere. At 36, tried for shooting at horses. His case has not been fully followed ; whether he reforms is to be tested, but the probabilities are against it, as he is living with a licentious woman.

Case 35. Passing to the cousins of these men, from lines 22 to 32, the career of the oldest has not been traced. Line 25, we find at 12 assisting his brother in a burglary ; at 17 serves two years in State prison for burglary ; at 22 two more years for breach of the peace, no doubt the severity of the sentence being made to cover two indictments for burglary which could not be proved, but which he no doubt committed ; at 24, burglary third degree, Sing Sing 3 years. It is said that the total years of imprisonment he has served in Pennsylvania, New Jersey, Vermont, and Rhode Island, has been from 13 to 14 years. In Clinton prison he learned iron rolling and also industrious habits, for now he has moved to another county, rents a quarry, and employs men to get out flag-stones. Here, again, before the meridian of life is passed, the education of labor, together with the experience of a riper age, produce an amended career.

Case 36. Line 26, brother of the above, at 20 years, county jail 30 days for assault and battery ; at 21, county jail 30 days for same offense ; at 22 Sing Sing two years for burglary third degree ; at 31 he moved into the same county as his brother above mentioned, purchased a farm and works a quarry upon it ; is worth $5,000 at 37, and the testimony of persons who have known him is, that "he is considerable of a man."

This line of facts points to two main lessons ; the value of labor as an element of reform, especially when we consider that the majority of the individuals of the " Juke " blood, when they work at all, are given to intermittent industries. The element of continuity is lacking in their character ; enforced labor in some cases seems to have the effect of supplying this deficiency. But the fact which is quite as important but less obvious, is, that crime and honesty run in the lines of greatest vitality, and that the qualities which make contrivers of crime are substantially the same as will make men successful in honest pursuits. In all the cases above cited burglary preponderates. This crime requires a strong physique, a cool head, and a good judgment backed by pluck. All these are qualities essential to any successful career, and the reform of these four men simply shows there is such a thing as interchangeability of careers, the solution of the problem of reform being how a new direction may be given to the activity of the faculties which are employed in a bad one. Indeed, so true is this view believed to be it is safe to venture the position that all criminals of sound mind and body who commit crimes of contrivance and who have not passed the meridian of life can be reformed, if only judicious training is applied in time. Where there is vitality, there morality can be organized and made a constituent part of character.

With criminals, gambling and licentiousness are widely prevalent. Any method which would direct this wasted power into other directions would produce an amended career. The problem amounts to this : given a certain amount of vitality, how shall it be expended so that the community shall not suffer injury. If, by training, evil modes should be closed up, not only could the energy be used for other purposes, but it would be so used, for life is activity of some sort, and will assert itself by effort of some kind.

What of the pauper? With him there is less hope, because less vitality, and less impressibility to praise or blame, to example or ambition. There also is, almost invariably, found licentiousness in some form. Here we have a key to solving some of the difficulties of his case. Virility is a mark of vitality, and sexual licentiousness, when unallied with disease, an index that there is yet vital strength, while reticence is a mark of power, for it indicates the subjection of the passions to the dominion of the will, storing up the vital forces, so to speak, for expenditure in other directions. Hard, continuous labor checks the erotic passion, prevents waste of vitality, tends to decrease its intensity by disuse, and in the course of time may enable the potential pauper to form habits of industry that will yet become organized as part of his character, and prove that pauperism can be controlled by controlling the passion which, disease aside, tends more than all other causes put together to perpetuate it hereditarily.

The Formation of Character.—Where there is heredity of any characteristic, it would seem there is a tendency, and it might almost be said, a certainty to produce an environment for the next generation corresponding to that heredity, with the effect of perpetuating it. Where the environment changes in youth the characteristics of heredity may be measurably altered. Hence the importance of education. In treating the subject it must be clearly understood and practically accepted, that the whole question of the educational management of crime, vice, and pauperism rests strictly and fundamentally upon a physiological basis, and not upon a sentimental or a metaphysical one. These phenomena take place not because there is any aberration in the laws of nature, but in consequence of the operation of these laws; because disease, because unsanitary conditions, because educational neglects, produce arrest of cerebral development at some point, so that the individual fails to meet the exigencies of the civilization of his time and country, and that the cure for unbalanced lives is a training which will affect the cerebral tissue, producing a corresponding change of career. This process of atrophy, physical and social, is to be met by methods that will remove the disabilities which check the required cerebral growth, or where the modification to be induced is profound, by the cumulative effect of training through successive generations under conditions favorable to such strengthening.

We have seen that disease in the parent will produce idiocy in the child ; this is arrest of cerebral development : that it will cause early death ; this is arrest of development. Besides these, arrest of development takes place in various other forms, at different stages and under widely differing circumstances. Excess of the passions prevents mental organization ; and neglected childhood even, produces the equivalent of arrest of development ; for, as in the case of the idiot, the arrest of cerebral development is caused by want of alimentary nutrition to the brain, so in the untaught child we get arrest of cerebral development caused by neglecting to furnish properly organized experience of the right relations of human beings to each other, which gives us a corresponding moral idiot.

Men do not become moral by intuition, but by patient organization and training. Indeed, the whole process of education consists of the building up of cerebral cells. For the purpose of a concise explanation, it may be said that there are four great subdivisions of the nervous system, each one of which presides over, co-ordinates and controls a separate set of functions. 1. The ganglionic nervous centres which connect the heart, lungs and internal viscera with each other and with the brain, bringing them into sympathetic action. 2. The spinal cord, which chiefly presides over the movements of the limbs and body. 3. The sensational centres, which register the impressions gathered by the senses. 4. The ideational centres, that enable us to reason, to think, to will, and, with this last, the moral nature. The ganglionic centres are, in a certain sense, subordinate to the spinal nerve centres ; these, in their turn, are subordinate to the sensory centres ; and these last are subordinate to the controlling action of the hemispheres of the brain, " and, especially to the action of the will, which, properly fashioned, represents the governing power of the voluntary actions." * While the mind is the last in order of development, it is the first in importance, and " instead of mind being a wondrous entity, the independent source of power and self-sufficient cause of causes, an honest observation proves incontestibly that it is the most dependent of all natural forces. It is the highest development of force, and to its existence all the lower natural forces are indispensably prerequisite." † This all-important will does not usually reach its full growth till between the thirtieth to the thirty-third years, and " is entirely dependent for its outward realization upon that mechanism of automatic action which is gradually organized in the subordinate centres—the cultivation of the senses are necessary antecedents to the due formation and operation of the will." ‡ We must therefore distinctly accept as an established

---

* Maudsley, Physiology and Pathology of the Mind, pp. 54, 55.
† Id. 60.   ‡ Id. 92, 93.

educational axiom, that the moral nature—which really means the holding of the emotions and passions under the dominion of the judgment by the exercise of will—is the last developed of the elements of character, and, for this reason, is most modifiable by the nature of the environment.

Leaving this branch of the inquiry we now come to the consideration of some of the English experience in the study of crime which bears on this question. Dr. Neison,* classifying the total population of England and Wales so as to divide them into successive terms of life as follows, from 10 to 15, from 15 to 20, from 20 to 25, from 25 to 30, from 30 to 40, from 40 to 50, from 50 to 60, found that age affected the tendency to crime in a remarkable degree. The maximum proportion of male criminals he found between the ages of 20 and 25, where the percentage of crime, as compared to the total male population of the same age, is .77.02 per cent, while between 50 and 60 the percentage to total population of the same age is only .16.94 per cent. Also the same law holds good for women but in different ratios, and here the tendency to crime at each successive term of life above enumerated decreases from 20 years at the rate of 33.333 per cent for males and 25 per cent for females. Now this gradual decrease is precisely what might be expected from the operation of the law of cerebral development above explained. From 15 to 20 the emotions and sensations are more active proportionately than they are at a later age. It is not that temptation is stronger, but that the will has not yet become fully organized, and therefore fails to govern the conduct. The formation of the character up to this time has been largely through precept and example ; experience has not yet come to teach, in its fulness, that a present self-denial may lead to a future greater advantage. But after twenty the formation of the character depends more upon experience, for the man of 25 does not find the same excuse granted for his misdeeds that the lad of 20 did ; the will now begins to be organized under what might be called social compulsion so as to become an efficient factor in conduct, and as it gradually strengthens by wider experience, the grown man sees the short-

---

* F. G. P. Neison, Vital Statistics, p. 404.

sighted policy of a criminal career and accommodates himself to social requirements.

This demonstrates that the natural process of the development of nerve tissue is a spontaneous and enormous force, capable of assisting in the work of reforming vicious and criminal lives. So long as there is growth, there can you produce change. Per contra, wherever you can change the environment so that the sensations, the experience, the habit of steady attention become automatic, you have at your disposal the means by which this will can be so developed, organized and made steady, that it can serve as a guide and as a restraint in the future career of the person so transferred to new environment. Here is the probable explanation of the spontaneous reform of the criminals whose cases are recited above. In spite of early training which was vicious ; in spite of our penal servitude, which is execrable, and not in consequence of it, we find that the disadvantages of criminal life have been weighed against the advantages of liberty and good repute, and a new course adopted after the twenty-fourth year, without any adventitious encouragement from reformatory institutions. The law would seem to be that development is in the direction of least resistance. Hence the value of good environment and the power of skilful training which removes obstacles to sound physical and mental organization and to an extent artificially contrives to open up the direction of least resistance in the channel of the established laws of social order.

But the statistical proof of a steady decrease of crime among males of 33 per cent for every term after 20 years of age, which, it has just been argued, is accounted for by growth of the will up to maturity, does not account for the decrease after that time. The facts collected in this report show that the essential characteristic of aggressive crime in the meridian of life is vitality ; that imprisonment causes and hastens induced pauperism ; and as life wanes the criminal tends to become a permanent public charge. Thus we get a gradual substitution of careers, from the criminal to the pauper, which glide into each other in so natural and steady a procession, that the ratio of decrease in crime, according to successive terms, as pointed out by Dr. Neison, is progressively continued to the end of life. We must not lose sight of a very important element in this connection. Although we have very little positive knowledge of the death-rate among criminals, we do know that fatal diseases are much more prevalent among them than with the average of men, and the great number of orphans in their ranks indicate how large a proportion of them are probably short lived by inheritance. But this inherited brevity of life and this diseased condition, we have already found, are merely the physiological aspect of what we call pauperism in its social aspect, and premature death is merely its terminal point. We may say, therefore, for convenience, that the ratio of decrease in crime at successive periods is affected by death, pauperism and reform, the degree of importance which they respectively play being in the order stated.

Intermittent industry.—After disease, the most uniformly noticeable trait of the true criminal is that he lacks the element of continuity of effort. Steady, plodding work, which is the characteristic not only of honest and successful individuals, but also of all nations that have made a mark in history, is deficient in him, and needs to be organized as a constituent of his character.

Max was "a hunter and a fisher," and in his industrial habits he is not only the type of his descendants but the organizer of their unfavorable condition. The great mass of them are of the grade of laborers, engaged in what may be called intermittent industries. Of the whole number of men, not 20 are skilled workmen, and of these, 10 have learned their trades in State prison. The industries which most of the "Jukes" pursued leave from three to four months of idle time during the winter season. Idleness results, and they rely on town help to pull through or take to tramping. This fluctuating state is full of dangers, and tends to perpetuate their social condition, which leads to the question of industrial training.

Industrial training.—We have seen that disease produces a deadening effect upon the moral sense, that intemperance results largely from some form of waning vitality, actual or potential ; that pauperism is due to the same process, and that the career of the criminal frequently begins and ends in the poor-house, the middle of life, when the vitality is strongest, being devoted to depredations. Behind all this, and in a certain sense antedating it, is fornication, speading diseases that undermine the vital force and literally create the idleness which is fortified by the cessation of work, so that both surroundings and proclivities become cumulative. The residuary vital force having ceased to be expended in labor, must find another mode of activity, and the one which presents itself as the most alluring is sexual excess, which thus completes a vicious circle, making idleness and fornication reciprocal causes of each other as hereditary characteristics which can only be eliminated from society by the advent of uncompromising death—the wages of sin. The argument for early marriage previously alluded to is strengthened by the fact that it brings with it the cares and obligations of rearing the family, and this is labor both physical and mental, which has a salutary effect in this respect upon women as well as upon men.

In the training of certain idiots, one of the great impediments in ameliorating their condition is found in the sexual orgasms to which they are addicted, the practice of which perpetuates their idiocy. The first step in improvement is to check their vice, and the main reliance to this end is occupation for mind and muscle, medication being only an auxiliary. In the institutions for the training of these unfortunates they are constrained to activity of some kind, their inert limbs are made to move, sometimes by the nurse, sometimes by mechanical contrivances which compel the flexion of the members, and their senses are gradually developed by being arbitrarily excited in a way appropriate to their nature. The result of this close, continuous and systematic turning of their attention to objects of the external world, unfolds their stunted minds, and produces fatigue, so that when laid down they fall to sleep at once without chance of sexual abandonment. It is the duty of the nurse to assure that each evening, and be ready to occupy the patient on the moment of his waking. Without this there is no cure. The lesson is, that the expenditure of the vital force in the direction of occupation subtracts just so much from sexual indulgence and reduces it to healthy periodicity.

The direct effect of industrial training is to curb licentiousness, its secondary effects to decrease the craving for stimulants and narcotics, to reduce the number of neglected children, to stimulate new sets of wants which will express themselves in a higher standard of living, and, concomitantly, promote the habits of industry which will enable those wants to be satisfied, thus completing a healthful circle in which labor and abstinence will become reciprocal causes of each other as hereditary characteristics which will promote longevity and enjoyment. In this way the log huts and hovels which now form hot-beds where human maggots are spawned, will disappear In their stead will be erected houses that will admit of separate sleeping apartments for the sexes, the mental attributes will gradually develop, æsthetic tastes take the place of debauchery, and a new social equilibrium be established.

How is this change to be effected ? In the first place, we have seen what a powerful agency is environment in determining the career ; therefore, any child of habitually criminal parents should be withdrawn from the influence of such a home, and the younger the child, after it is weaned, the better the chances of success. In the second place, the family is the fundamental type of social organization, and, as we found it was necessary to take the family in its successive generations as the only proper basis for a study of our subject, so have we found, in those cases where the established order of society has spontaneously produced amended lives, that the family hearth has formed an essential point of departure.* Accepting this as a lesson and a model, any institution that proposes to deal with the reformation of delinquents must adopt some scheme which shall embody this fundamental relationship, remembering that love of home and pride in it are the most powerful motives in checking vagrancy, and in organizing the environnent that can perpetuate these essential domestic sentiments.

When the term "industrial training" is used, much more is meant than formal instruction in a trade. It is contemplated that, in a properly ordered scheme of reformation, something like a general training of the faculties must be provided for. Our Reformatories must reform and develop the senses of touch, hearing, sight, smell and taste, so that the mind shall be filled with the knowledge of things, instead

---

* See cases 3, 6, 36.

of being left vacant of everything except a memorizing of words. With the use of the faculties will gradually be developed varieties of emotion and intelligence, which, tending to activities in their own direction, will reorganize the career of the individual so that criminal or vicious courses can be supplanted by automatic virtue. Every reformatory should take for its model of school training, either the kindergarten education or the method of object lessons, or some modification of these which is practicable, for the potential thief, if not a moral imbecile, is a moral infant. The advantage of the kindergarten instruction rests in this, that it coherently trains the senses and quickens the spirit of moral accountability, building them into cerebral tissue. It thus organizes new channels of activity through which vitality may spread itself for the advantage of the individual and the benefit of society, concurrently endowing each individual with a governing will. Such an energetic, judicious and thorough training of the children of our criminal population would, in fifteen years, show itself by the great decrease in the number of commitments, and at a less cost in money than their adult depredations. Such training is not to be found in our reformatories conducted upon the congregate system, and still less in our prisons, penitentiaries and jails.

Indeed, so conspicuous is the failure of the entire machinery of the punitive and reformatory institutions of our State, that we cannot call these establishments the results of the wisdom of our generation, but rather the cumulative accidents of popular negligence, indifference and incapacity. A survey of the field of reform, and of those to be saved, has profoundly shaken my faith in the sufficiency of any mere institution, as an agent to reform the erring, without the active co-operation of the public.

Tentative Inductions in Reform.

1. The formation of character depends upon an orderly and well-defined development of faculty from youth to maturity.

2. This development is a spontaneous force capable of facilitating reform.

3. This metamorphosis operates most powerfully in the moral field from the twenty-third to the thirty-first year.

4. It partially explains the proportionate decrease of crime in successive terms of life, as shown by Dr. Neison.

5. With the advance of age the effects of imprisonment and disease cumulate. They produce induced pauperism which acts as a substitution of careers, from criminal to pauper condition.

6. This accounts for another portion of the decrease of crime ratio among criminals.

7. The vices of criminals so disease them that the average death-rate is raised, and this rate increases in an accelerated ratio, especially from the thirty-fifth year.

8. This explains another proportionate decrease of crime.

There is another tendency among criminals that affects the proportionate decrease of crime, which it may be well to state here, although the evidence of it is not gathered from the " Jukes," but from the "Further Studies of Criminals," and is here stated.

9. That the tendency of many criminals from the age of twenty-five is to change from executors of crimes to contrivers of the same, from the thirty-fifth to the forty-fifth to become crime capitalists or the keepers of liquor shops or brothels where crimes are planned. They thus measurably avoid arrest and imprisonment.

10. Reform is more probable with adult criminals than adult paupers.

11. The law of human development is in the direction of least resistance.*

12. Effective methods of reform require that obstacles to sound physical and mental organization should be removed, so that the direction of least resistance shall, by artificial design, be opened up in the channels of social order.

13. The " Jukes " are conspicuous for lack of continuity of effort

---

* When I first made this statement in the edition of 1875, I thought it was new to me. During a visit to Dr. E. Van de Warker, of Syracuse, the subject of the direction of least resistance came up in conversation. Then I recollected that I was indebted to Mr. Herbert Spencer for the idea. Many years ago I had read his *Physiology of Laughter*, and had forgotten it so completely that, unconsciously, I adapted the illustration of the distribution of nervous force contained in that essay to the explanation of the social phenomena I was comparing—the relations of harlotry, pauperism and crime.

and for precocious sexual excitability which are both of them such obstacles.

14. These two features react on each other as cause and effect, stimulate crime and induce pauperism.

15. The foundation of their education should be sexual training from early childhood.

16. This involves, 1st, Separation from contaminating example to control the moral environment : 2d, Industrial training with culture of the æsthetic tastes.

17. Separation from parents should be secured by placing the children to be so trained in good families or in institutions that are conducted on the *family system.*

18. The culture and industrial training are best secured by "Kindergarten education."

Institutional life, which helps to break down the self-reliance of inmates, must be superseded by dispersion into good families.　I now have in mind an extensive employer of labor, located near the original settlement of the "Jukes," and who employs several members of it.　His rule is to treat them with firmness and unvaryingly scrupulous fairness.　He never swerves from what he says, never evades a promise made.　This establishes over them an empire that makes them trust him, and when they get into difficulties, they come to him for advice.　He acts as their banker, encourages them to save, and in the case of boys from 13 to 15, who have formed acquaintance of licentious women, he interposes his authority and checks their career of licentiousness by establishing a bond of mutual good faith between himself and the offender, the latter promising to discontinue his courses if his former conduct is not reported to his parents.　In this way an ascendency is gained that tends to check many an incipient crime ; but he never lets his relations with them fall into the weakness of patronage.　He is school trustee, and where widows depend upon their boys for support, he arranges that they shall work for him, and go to school alternate weeks.　He has not taken up this work as a "mission," but strictly as a business man, who, finding himself placed where he must employ the rude laborers of his locality, deals with them on the sound and healthy basis of commercial contract, honesty carried out and rigidly enforced.

It is such a class of employers who are needed to deal with the criminally inclined ; men who understand human nature, rightly estimate the lack of social opportunity which encompasses a population of " Jukes," and can make allowances for the shortcomings and frailties of a class who are less evil in nature than they are untrained in conduct. If such prudent persons could be enlisted in the work, they would prove the most efficient of all reformers, because reform would be secured under liberty, the only ultimate test of self-balance.

1. *Tentative Generalizations on Heredity and Environment.*— Where the organization is structurally modified, as in idiocy and insanity, or organically weak as in many diseases, the heredity is the preponderating factor in determining the career ; but it is, even then, capable of marked modification for better or worse by the character of the environment. In other words, capacity, physical and mental, is limited and determined mainly by heredity. This is probably because it is fixed during the period of ante-natal organization.

2. Where the conduct depends on the knowledge of moral obligation (excluding insanity and idiocy), the environment has more influence than the heredity, because the development of the moral attributes is mainly a post-natal and not an ante-natal formation of cerebral cells. The use to which capacity shall be put is largely governed by the impersonal training or agency of environment, which is itself very variable.

3. The tendency of heredity is to produce an environment which perpetuates that heredity : thus, the licentious parent makes an example which greatly aids in fixing habits of debauchery in the child. The correction is change of environment. For instance, where hereditary kleptomania exists, if the environment should be such as to become an exciting cause, the individual will be an incorrigible thief ; but if, on the contrary, he be protected from temptation, that individual may lead an honest life, with some chances in favor of the entailment stopping there.

E

4. Environment tends to produce habits which may become hereditary, especially so in pauperism and licentiousness, if it should be sufficiently constant to produce modification of cerebral tissue.

If these conclusions are correct, then the whole question of the control of crime and pauperism become possible, within wide limits, if the necessary training can be made to reach over two or three generations.

5. From the above considerations the logical induction seems to be, that environment is the ultimate controlling factor in determining careers, placing heredity itself as an organized result of invariable environment. The permanence of ancestral types is only another demonstration of the fixity of the environment within limits which necessitate the development of typal characteristics.

Extension of the field of Genealogical study.—The "Jukes" take in only a fraction of the domain of investigation into crime, its cause and cure. The essential characteristics of the group are great vitality, ignorance and poverty. They have never had a training which would bring into activity the æsthetic tastes, the habits of reasoning, or indeed a desire for the ordinary comforts of a well-ordered home. They are not an exceptional class of people : their like may be found in every county in this State. For this reason an exhaustive analysis of this family is valuable, because the inductions drawn from their careers are applicable to a numerous and widely disseminated class who need to be reached by similar agencies.

The study here presented is largely tentative, and care should be taken that the conclusions drawn be not applied indiscriminately to the general questions of crime and pauperism, for we are here dealing mainly with blood relations living in a similar environment, physical, social and governmental, in whom the order of events noted may be hereditary characteristics special to themselves, and not of unvarying recurrence.

Nevertheless, it opens the way and supplies the method for a study of other cases, supplementing and complementing this one, and presenting a different point of departure, whether it be the progeny of influential landed proprietors who lapse into pauperism, or the children of people of culture and refinement who become felons ; or again, of the converse of these, of children whose parents were criminals, and yet have re-entered the ranks of the repuable.

Different kinds of crime need special study. Thus crimes of contrivance in their various forms, as burglary, embezzlement ; crimes of education, as forgery ; crimes of brutality, as malicious mischief and murder ; crimes of cunning, as pocket picking, false pretenses ; crimes of weakness, crimes of debauchery, crimes of ambition, crimes of riches, crimes of disease. Pauperism also needs a series, and this and crime need to be compared to each other, and, respectively, to a third series, investigating the growth and permanence of generations morally developed. The study of human nature thus pursued would give us a classified variety of characters, conditions and tendencies covering gradations so perfectly distributive that we could take any typical case, follow from this as a central point in any direction and note the shades of change which lead to other typical cases and so get a right conception of the continuity and essential unity of sociological phenomena, and perhaps discover a law of social equivalents. Such a series would form a body of evidence which would furnish data enabling us to pronounce judgment upon any scheme put forth to counteract the increase of crime, and supplant the empirical method now in vogue, by one of exact and well-founded laws, derived from a patient and extensive study of the phenomena involved.

Having discussed the elements of the subject, the various parts are presented (table XI.) in a statistical aggregate. The line headed "Marriageable Age" will give, very nearly, the number of adults in each generation : girls of 14 and boys of 18 are included under that heading.

The social damage of the " Jukes " estimated.—Passing from the actual record, I submit an estimate of the damage of the family, based on what is known of those whose lives have been learned. The total number of persons included in the foregoing statement reach 709 ; besides these, 125 additional names have been gathered since

the text of this *essay* was prepared, whose general character is
similar.   If all the collateral lines which have not been traced could
be added to the 709 here tabulated, the aggregate would reach at
least 1,200 persons, living and dead.   Now, out of 700 persons we
have 180 who have either been to the poor-house or received out-
door relief to the extent of 800 years.   Allowing that the best
members of the family have emigrated, it would be a low estimate
to say that 80 of the additional 500 are, or have been, dependents,
adding 350 years to the relief, making an aggregate of 280 persons
under pauper training, receiving 1,150 years of public charity.
Great as this is, it is not all.   In a former portion of this report, it
was stated the pauper records cover 255 years, of which only 64
could be consulted, the difficulties of getting the remaining 191
years being, in most cases, insuperable.   Allowing that these 191
years would yield as many years of relief as the 64 which have actually been searched, we should have an aggregate of 2,300 years of
out-door relief.   Allowing 150 years of alms-house life at $100 a
year, the sum expended equals $15,000, and for 2,150 years of out-
door relief, at the moderate rate of $15 a year, $32,250, making an
aggregate expenditure of $47,250 in 75 years for this single family,
52 per cent of whose women are harlots in some degree.   Making
a like computation for the other items of the schedule, allowing for
all contingencies a financial estimate may be summed up as
follows :

		COST
Total number of persons	1,200	....
Number of pauperized adults	280	....
Cost of alms-house relief	....	$15,000 .00
Cost of out-door relief	....	32,250.00
Number of criminals and offenders	140	....
Years of imprisonment	140	....
Cost of maintenance, at $200 a year	....	28,000.00
Number of arrests and trials	250	....
Cost of arrests and trials, $100 each	....	25,000.00
Number of habitual thieves, convicted and unconvicted	60	... .
Number of years of depredation, at 12 years each	720	....
Cost of depredation, $120 a year	....	86,400.00
Number of lives sacrificed by murder	7	....·

TABLE XI.—STATISTICAL SUMMARY OF THE "JUKES."

		Parentage by Sex			Marriage Relations											Property			Pauperism				Crime		
Generation	Total number in generation	Total each sex	Legitimate	Illegitimate	Marriageable age	Unmarried adults	Married	Had bastards before marriage	Had bastards after marriage	Prostitutes	Unascertained	Barren persons	Kept brothels	Syphilis	Acquired	Lost	Out-door relief, No. persons	No. of years	Alms-house, No. persons	No. of years	No. of persons	No. of years	No. of offenses
2d Gen. Juke women	5	5	1		5		5	3		3		5		1	1		3	20	2	2			
X men	5	5	2	1	5	2	5			3				1				23					
3d Gen. Juke women	34	16	15		16		13	1	1	3	1	4	5	12	4	1		54	3	6		3	1
X women		7	3	6	7	6	4			3	1		1	7	1	1		14	3	5			2
Juke men		18	18		18		11							6									
X men	16	9	12	2	9	5	5			4	5		8	2									
4th Gen. Juke women	117	46	38	1	39	10	26	6	8	12	6	8	5		5	3	18	122	7	7	5	1	7
X women		25	6		25		15			4		4					8	53	3	3	2		2
Juke men		57	46	8	54	14	22	3			23	7					19	129	8	12	12	11	15
X men	59	34	5	1	34		19			15		1			2	1	11	50	3	3	10	13	11
5th Gen. Juke women	224	119	94	17	90	8	37	6	3	36	7	5	2	25	5	1	24	100	12	18	9		15
X women		4	4		33		21	2	1	14	4	4		2			11	49	2	4	1		1
Juke men		102	70		69	1	15			12	22	7		7	3	1	25	87	11	21	18	72	41
X men	84	51	11	3	51		26			14	11	6		4			14	33			12	8	16
6th Gen. Juke women	152	63	33	13	12		2	2		2	1		1				4		3	8	2		2
X women		2			1		1										5						
Juke men		48	27	20	2		1	1		1							20		7	7	2		2
X men	5	3			3		2										7						
7th Gen. Juke women	8	3	1	2	3																		
Juke men										1			1										
Tot. Gen. Juke women	540	252	188	33	162	26	83	18	12	53	8	13	11	37	15		45	242	24	35	16	13¾	24
X women		67	13	3	67		35	6	1	21	12	8	1	9			20	125	5	7	3		3
Juke men		225	155	49	143	20	55			20	50	18	1	14	14	5	50	270	29	46	33	89¾	69
X men	169	102	18	6	102		57			34	19	7	5	7	7	3	27	97	6	8	24	24	29
Juke blood	540	477	337	82	305	46	138	18	12	73	58	31	12	51	15	5	95	512	53	81	49	91¾	83
X blood	169	169	31	9	169	46	92	6	1	55	23	15	6	16	7	3	47	222	11	15	27	24¼	32
Grand total.	709	645	368	91	474	46	230	24	13	128	81	46	18	67	22	8	142	734	64	96	76	116	115

		COST.
Value, at $1,200 each..	....	$8,400.00
Number of common prostitutes...................................	50	....
Average number of years of debauch.............................	15	....
Total number of years of debauch...............................	750	....
Cost of maintaining each per year......................... ....$300.00		....
Cost of maintenance...	....	225,000.00
Number of women specifically diseased..........................	40	....
Average number of men each woman contaminates with permanent disease...	 10	....
Total number of men contaminated..............................	400	....
Number of wives contaminated by above men....................	40	....
Total number of persons contaminated..........................	440	....
Cost of drugs and medical treatment during rest of life, at $200 each	....	88,000.00
Average loss of wages caused by disease during rest of life, in years	3	....
Total years of wages lost by 400 men...........................	1,200	....
Loss, at $500 a year...	....	600,000.00
Average number of years withdrawn from productive industry by each courtesan..	10	....
Total number of years lost by 50 courtesans....................	500	....
Value estimated at $125 a year................................	....	62,500.00
Aggregate curtailment of life of 490 adults, equivalent to 50 mature individuals..	50	....
Cash cost, each life at $1,200.................................	....	60,000.00
Aggregate of children who died prematurely....................	300	....
Average years of life of each child............................	2	....
Cash cost, each child at $50...................................	....	15,000.00
Number of prosecutions in bastardy............................	30	....
Average cost of each case, $100...............................	....	3,000.00
Cost of property destroyed, blackmail, brawls *................	....	20,000.00
Average capital employed in houses, stock, furniture, etc., for brothels..	....	6,000.00
Compound interest for 26 years at 6 per cent...................	....	18,000.00
Charity distributed by church.................................	....	10,000.00
Charity obtained by begging...................................	....	5,450.00
Total...	....	$1,308,000.00

Over a million and a quarter dollars of loss in 75 years, caused
by a single family 1,200 strong, without reckoning the cash paid for
whiskey, or taking into account the entailment of pauperism and
crime of the survivors in succeeding generations, and the incurable
disease, idiocy and insanity growing out of this debauchery, and
reaching further than we can calculate. It is getting to be time to
ask, do our courts, our laws, our alms-houses and our jails deal with
the question presented ?

---

* One house, with furniture worth $1,100, was burned by a mob.

II.

FURTHER STUDIES OF CRIMINALS.

STATE—PRISON CONVICTS.

THE State of New York has enacted thirty statutes or parts of statutes which relate to the collection, accuracy, and preservation of the statistics of crime, the administration of criminal justice, the finances of penal institutions, the identification of the criminal classes, and the indenture, conduct and fate of minors who have been placed in reformatories. There are at least nineteen distinct classes of officers upon whom is imposed some part of the duty of making these returns correct, or of preserving them when they are reported to the proper officers, according to the provisions of law. Before making an examination of the convicts in the prisons of this State, which was ordered by resolution of the Association June 24, 1875, it was thought advisable to examine the statistics which the law has made such elaborate provisions to collect, so that the inquiry might rest upon postulates indicating the right direction of study and establish standards for the comparisons of associated facts. For this purpose, the registers of State prisons and penitentiaries, the returns of county magistrates, the records of jails and of county clerks, and the archives of the Secretary of State have been examined, only to find that nothing exists sufficiently reliable to serve in the study of crime or the movements of crime classes, and that a beginning must be made from the foundation. The provisions of the law itself are so incongruous that no just comparisons can be instituted, even if every officer should make an exact return according to the statute, for the schedules differ widely, the reports are made to different officers, so that they are not gathered into one central office, and the responsibility for neglecting to make returns is in some cases dubious. Aside from these statutory defects, there are other causes which greatly add to the faultiness of criminal statistics, and may be divided into four general categories : First, the inefficiency of the police ; second, the defects in the administration of justice ; third, the falsification and defectiveness of the records ; and, fourth, public apathy.

Under the first we have : First, the undetected, who commit crimes and evade punishment by covering their iniquities from public knowledge. Among this class may be found defaulters, guardians who appropriate trust funds, abortionists, various panderers to vices and receivers of stolen goods, who are protected by the craft because they are crime capitalists. Second, the unarrested who are represented by those who either have evaded or made terms with the police, or who live in the rural districts where practically no police exists ; also, such depredators as private individuals decline to appear against, either from indifference, from intimidation, or by compounding their felonies.

Coming under the category of defects in the administration of justice we have : First, the unprosecuted, a very large band who get off either by *nolle prosequi* or by giving straw bail. Second, the unjustly acquitted by sympathizing juries or other means. Third, the acceptance of pleas of guilty of a minor offense when a major one has been committed. Fourth, the convictions for constructive crime, by giving the evidence against a prisoner an interpretation which allows prosecution for a greater offense than that actually committed, as where robbery from a woman is construed into attempt at rape. Fifth, the immunity of those who turn State's evidence against their confederates. In these ways we fail to get at the actual quality of the crime—for in a vast number of convictions there has been no trial—we only get the name of certain offenses which do not have even the merit of being accurately defined.

As to the defectiveness and falsification of records, these are very numerous : First, The neglect of country justices to transmit duplicate copies of commitments and finable cases to county clerks, as required by law. In some counties, not one-fourth of the cases adjudged are reported, and in almost every county they are defective. So far is this kind of negligence carried that we have found men locked up in jail without a *mittimus*. Second, The neglect of many sheriffs to keep jail registers, and the consequent inability to make returns to the Secretary of State of the persons committed to the county jail for offenses punishable by imprisonment in such prisons. Third, The neglect of county clerks to furnish correct monthly returns of the indictments and sentences in courts of record to the Secretary of State. Fourth, The negligence of clerks in transcribing copies of returns. Fifth, The mutilation of the records of the courts of record, successive pages being in some instances bodily cut out. Sixth, The failure to identify habitual criminals, so that we know absolutely nothing of the proportion of first offenders to habitual criminals. One man, aged forty-one, who figures on the records as committed for second offense, began prison life at seven years of age, has been twice in the house of refuge, once in the juvenile asylum, and altogether sixteen times in prisons of some degree (mostly penitentiary), each time committed from New York city. Another, aged seventy-four years, who also appears on the registers of a State prison as committed for second offense, is now serving his seventh consecutive term in the same prison in which this registry is made, the sum of his united sentences amounting to seventeen years. Out of 233 cases examined, 79.40 per cent are undoubtedly habitual criminals ; of these only twenty-six per cent are registered upon the books as such. Seventh, The falsification of ages, names, nativities, by convicts, to protect themselves in various ways from severe sentences. Boys of sixteen give their ages as nineteen, because they do not want to be sent to the house of refuge ; while others of nineteen give their ages as sixteen, because they do. In Buffalo and Albany, offenders give their ages as older, so as to be sent to State prison instead of the Penitentiary, because " you get better food and less work to do ; " but in New York city they give ages younger than the facts, preferring to go to Blackwell's Island, " because there you don't work and you get shorter time." Many give false names, because their own is too notorious, or to protect their relations from disgrace, or to save themselves from the odium of appearing on prison registers, resuming their real names on discharge. Eighth, The registering, as facts, statements made by prisoners which are purely fictions. Thus, under the name "religious training," the convicts figure as Catholic or Protestant, when the most superficial examination demonstrates they are absolutely indifferent to either faith and equally ignorant of the tenets of both. Under the head "education," many are registered as "read and write" who can only write their name and can hardly spell, while under "social condition" the married are registered as single, those who have never lived in any other than illicit relations are registered as married, and under that ægis are allowed to write letters to their concubines serving sentence in the female prison or in some penitentiary, because the law allows correspondence only between man and wife.

There is therefore every possible variety of error to impair the value of what are called our criminal statistics. Under the circumstances, we can fully appreciate the candor of Gen. Francis A. Walker when he says, in his preface to the Statistics of Crime and Pauperism in United States Census for 1870 : * "The results are now submitted with the remark, that neither the statements of crime nor those of pauperism *for the year* are regarded as possessing any high degree of statistical authority." * * * Although "the numbers reported respectively as receiving poor support and as in prison *on the 1st of June*, 1870, are regarded as quite accurately determined."

In view of these facts, it was found necessary to make a tentative examination of the prisoners themselves, to get at some approximately correct data which might serve in the study of crime character, crime causes and the unfolding of crime careers. The numbers who have been examined, however, are too few to be accepted as finally conclusive statistics upon the subject ; but they prove how entirely practicable it is to get quite trustworthy information on a very wide range of inquiries covering the entire life of the individual, and on many points respecting his parentage and his relations.

---

* Vol. i., page 567.

To test to its fullest extent the possibility of gathering such materials, the following schedule was used in the examinations :

SCHEDULE USED IN THE EXAMINATION OF CONVICTS.

I. *Parental Antecedents.*

1. Are the parents consanguineous.—What degree ?—2. What has been the family example of father and mother as to temperance, industry, chastity, debauchery, pauperism, crime, education, religion ; also property, trade, present age, age at death, disease?—3. Has he criminal uncles, aunts or cousins, and how many ?

II. *Personal History.*

4. Legitimate birth.—5. Color.—6. Age.—7. Single.—8. Married.—9. Divorced.—10. Widowed.—11. Illicit relation.—12. Number of children, boys, girls, legitimate, illegitimate.—13. Homeless childhood by abandonment of father, mother, by death of father, mother, by imprisonment of father, mother, by pauperism of father, mother.—14. Was other guardian provided ?—15. Was it a kinsman, a stranger, an institution ?—16. Character of guardian.—17. How many brothers and sisters had he ?—18. Their order of birth ?

III. *Pauperism.*

19. What form ?—Poor-house.—Out-door relief.—Vagrancy.—20. At what age ?—21. How long ?—22. How did home get unfixed?—By death of. — Abandonment of. — Imprisonment of.—Want of work.—Loss of property.

IV. *Industrial Training.*

23. Industrious.—24. Lazy.—25. Apprenticed. — 26. Served . . . . years.—27. What trade.—28. Profession ?—29. Was it fully learned ?—30. Why not ?—31. How much time lost since ?—32. Use of spare time.—33. Character of companions.—34. Where he met them.—35. How many of them since convicted ?—Sent to State prison.—36. Ever in army.—Kept rum shop.—37. Or brothel.

V. *Education.*

38. Reads.—39. Writes.—40. Cyphers.—41. Common school education.—Years.—Truant.—42. Higher education.—Its degree. —43. Accomplishments.—44. Intelligence.—45. Useful knowledge. —46. Ignorant.—47. Stolid.

VI. *Religious Training and Moral Traits.*

48. Moral sense.—49. Realizes criminal nature of offense committed.—50. Acknowledges obligations to Divine law.—51. What denomination?—52. Dominant traits.

VII. *Physical and Mental Characteristics.*

53. General health.—54. Constitutional temperament.—55. Appearance of countenance.—Head.—Skin.—Eyes.—Posture.—Gait. —56. Blind.—Deaf and dumb.—Malformed.—Injured.—Insane.— Paralyzed.—Mentally defective. — 57. Description of sane.— 58. Cause.—59. Consequences.—60. Age when first symptoms appeared.—61. General feebleness of mind.—62. General feebleness of body.—63. Moral perversion leading to morbid practices.—64. What practices.—65. Diseases.—Nervous.—Chorea.—Epilepsy.— Insomnia.—Hallucinations.

Other diseases—Constitutional.—Respiratory system.—Circulatory system.—Nutritive system.—Osseous system.—Generative and urinary organs.—66. Is it hereditary?

VIII. *Vices.*

67. Gambling.—68. Opium habit.—69. Prostitution. — When practiced first time.—70. How habit began.—71. Inebriety, occasional.—Periodical.—Habitual.—72. At what age was habit begun. —Fixed.—How long fixed.—73. Its effects.

IX. *Property.*

74. Has inherited property.—When.—75. Acquired property.— When.—76. Lost it.—When.—77. How lost.—Prisoner's name.— Offense.—Prison Register No.—List No.—Name of prison or penitentiary.—Date.

X. *Addresses.*

A table of addresses as follows :—Where born.—**Where resid-ing.**—Crime, where committed.—Where tried.—Person injured.—Best friend.—Worst enemy.—Family physician.—Birth-place, father.—Birth-place, mother.—Criminal haunts.—Came to United States in—

XI. *Criminal History.*

78. First seduction into culpable offense, what age ?—79. What necessity led to it ?—80. What temptation or agency ?—81. What vice or passion ?—82. What disease ?—83. Out of employment.—Sick.—84. What was the offense ?—85. First trial, at what age ?—Acquitted.—86. Innocent.—Guilty.—87. By what influence caused.—88. What necessity led to it ?—89. What temptation or agency ?—90. What vice or passion ?—91. Aggregate number of offenses be-fore first trial.—92. Total number of arrests.—93. Indictments pending.

XII. *Criminal Status.*

94. First offender.—95. Habitual criminal.—96. Contriver of crime.—97. What kind ?—98. At what age ?—99. On what scale ?

XIII. *Reformation.*

100. What is the probability of reform.—101. By what means ?—102. Needs industrial training.—103. Needs guidance.

XIV. *Criminal Commerce.*

104. Mode of business.—105. How was property disposed of ?—106. What is its aggregate value ?—107. Aggregate booty.—108. Aggregate offenses during career.—109. Largest steal.

XV. *Table of Imprisonments.*

Crime ?—When committed ? Article stolen, its value ?—If murder, what instrument ?—If rape, age of woman. — Sentence.—Name of prison.—Time served.

When this schedule was first used in the State Prisons, its employment was greatly discouraged by officials whose long acquaintance with criminals led them to believe that it would be impossible to get any correct information from the convicts. Indeed, so persistent were the representations that felons will rather lie than tell the truth, that I adopted the policy of informing each man that, if any question I asked involved an answer he did not wish to make, he might decline without having his reasons for so doing questioned. In addition, and as a test of accuracy and before credit was given to the statements thus made, the schedules of a certain number of convicts were verified by entering into correspondence with the officers of a number of institutions, with members of the local committees of this Association, and with the police of different cities. The result of these inquiries has been substantially to yield a useful study in human nature and to relieve the criminal class from an aspersion which it does not deserve. It is common to accept the legal assumption that if a man falsifies about one fact he will falsify about all facts. There is no such consistency in human nature ; the assumption is a legal fiction so far as criminals are concerned ; for, as a class, they do not falsify the truth except when they hope to gain something they desire, to hide something they fear, or to conceal some fact about themselves of which they are ashamed, in which respects they do not materially differ from the average man. Upon matters which they consider indifferent, their answers are as accurate as their knowledge extends, but on the questions relating to the number of their commitments or offenses, many declined to answer, although substantially admitting they were habitual criminals, and confessing their besetting crime. Another class of subjects which it was impossible to reach, about which only indirect questions were asked, was that relating to the good name of the mother and sisters. In only two cases have the convicts acknowledged the bad repute of their mothers, and in both cases it was given voluntarily. In both cases also it turns out that the men were serving terms for rape, and seemed to have absolutely no sense of honor about women, one of them being almost an imbecile.

The Statistical Results.

At Auburn 152 males and one female were examined, at Sing Sing ninety-two males and six females, a total of 251 persons. Of this number eighteen have been totally rejected. As each man was examined, whenever there was doubt as to the veracity or the intelligence of his reply, such answer was recorded on the schedule together with a note of interrogation, and when the tabulation was made, such answer was excluded. In this way a portion of one hundred of the schedules was thrown out, which explains why the following tables do not balance exactly in every item. These tables are strictly an enumeration of certain ascertained facts respecting the persons who were examined, and conform strictly to the requirements of *positive statistics*. They must not be used as a basis to reason on as to the relative frequency of different offenses, or to compute any ratios on any of the points they contain to be applied to the criminal class in general, because the numbers are insufficient, because they exclude offenders in penitentiaries and common jails, and because they represent a limited experience in only two State prisons (Sing Sing and Auburn), the effect of transferring convicts from these to Clinton prison being equivalent to the selection of certain ages and classes of convicts, so that a true average cannot be found in any one prison. The tables are constructed in such a manner that the total number under any one heading are in the black figures running diagonally across the table, the light figures on the same line giving the number in sub-headings. Thus in table I., habitual criminals 40, of whom 34 were sane, 6 of *neurotic* stock, 15 refuge boys, 33 no trade, &c., &c.

Table I.—Burglary.

Sane, 39—Neurotic Stock,* 9—Total, 48.

	Sane.	Neurotic stock.*	Orphans.	Not orphans.	Neglected children.	Habitual criminals.	First offenders.	Refuge boys.	Criminal family.	Pauper stock.	Intemperate family.	Habitual drunkards.	Temperate.	Reformable.	Hopeless.	Have trade.	No trade.
Orphans	16	3	19	..	10	17	2	8	2	8	5	4	5	8	9	1	18
Not orphans	23	6	..	29	18	23	6	7	8	8	11	12	5	14	9	7	21
Neglected children	23	5	10	18	28	24	3	13	5	11	12	9	8	10	12	2	24
Habitual criminals	34	6	17	23	24	40	..	15	9	12	15	16	5	17	16	6	33
First offenders	5	3	2	6	3	..	8	..	1	4	1	..	5	5	2	2	6
Refuge boys	12	3	8	7	13	15	..	15	2	6	6	5	2	3	7	1	13
Criminal family	6	4	2	8	5	9	1	2	10	4	4	3	..	4	2	2	7
Pauper stock	11	5	8	8	11	12	4	6	4	16	8	5	4	3	6	3	12
Intemperate family	11	5	5	11	12	15	1	6	4	8	16	11	2	3	5	1	10
Habitual drunkards	12	4	4	12	9	16	..	5	3	5	11	16	..	7	6	8	8
Temperate	7	3	5	5	8	5	5	2	..	4	2	..	10	2	5	1	7
Reformable	20	2	8	14	10	17	5	3	4	3	3	7	2	22	..	3	18
Hopeless	13	5	9	9	12	16	2	7	2	6	5	6	5	..	18	3	14
Have trade	5	3	1	7	2	6	2	1	2	3	1	8	1	3	3	8	..
No trade	33	6	18	21	24	33	6	13	7	12	10	8	7	18	4	..	39

TABLE II.—Larceny, Grand and Petit.

Sane, 71—Neurotic Stock, 13—Total, 84.

	Sane.	Neurotic stock.*	Orphans.	Not orphans.	Neglected children.	Habitual criminals.	First offenders.	Refuge boys.	Criminal family.	Pauper stock.	Intemperate family.	Habitual drunkards.	Temperate.	Reformable.	Hopeless.	Have trade.	No trade.
Orphans	35	1	36	..	24	31	5	4	6	11	16	17	6	12	11	8	28
Not orphans	36	12	..	48	19	37	10	11	5	8	19	16	5	18	16	15	33
Neglected childhood	34	6	24	19	40	36	3	12	7	10	21	16	4	15	14	8	32
Habitual criminals	59	9	31	37	36	68	..	15	9	16	27	30	7	22	24	19	49
First offenders	11	4	5	10	3	..	15	0	2	3	8	3	4	10	3	4	11
Refuge boys	12	3	4	11	12	15	0	15	3	3	7	5	2	5	7	6	9
Criminal family	9	2	6	5	7	9	2	3	11	2	6	3	2	6	2	2	9
Pauper stock	10	9	11	8	10	16	3	3	2	19	7	9	1	7	10	7	12
Intemperate family	28	7	16	19	21	27	8	7	6	7	35	13	11	4	11	6	28
Habitual drunkards	31	2	17	16	16	30	3	5	3	9	13	33	..	11	16	4	15
Temperate	11	0	6	5	4	7	4	2	2	1	11	..	11	8	0	3	8
Reformable	29	3	12	18	15	22	10	5	6	7	14	11	8	32	..	8	24
Hopeless	22	5	11	16	14	24	3	7	2	10	11	16	0	..	27	8	19
Have trade	17	6	8	15	8	19	4	6	2	7	6	4	3	8	8	23	..
No trade	54	7	28	33	32	49	11	9	9	12	28	15	8	24	19	..	61

* Under the term *neurotic stock*, in the following twelve tables, are included those who are descended from, related to by blood, or are themselves either idiotic, insane, epileptic, paralytic, or otherwise nervously disordered.

TABLE III.—LARCENY FROM PERSON.

Sane, 16—Neurotic Stock, 4—Total, 20.

	Sane.	Neurotic stock.	Orphans.	Not orphans.	Neglected childhood.	Habitual criminals.	First offenders.	Refuge boys.	Criminal family.	Pauper stock.	Intemperate family.	Habitual drunkards.	Temperate.	Reformable.	Hopeless.	Have trade.	No trade.
Orphans	7	1	**8**	..	5	6	2	4	1	0	5	4	1	5	0	4	4
Not orphans	9	3	..	**12**	11	11	1	8	4	4	8	7	2	6	3	3	9
Neglected childhood	13	3	5	11	**16**	14	2	11	5	4	11	9	1	10	3	5	11
Habitual criminals	15	2	6	11	14	**17**	..	11	5	4	10	9	2	10	3	5	12
First offenders	1	2	2	1	2	..	**3**	1	0	0	3	2	1	1	0	2	1
Refuge boys	11	1	4	8	11	11	1	**12**	3	3	7	6	1	8	1	6	6
Criminal family	3	2	1	4	5	5	0	3	**5**	1	2	3	0	2	3	2	3
Pauper stock	3	1	0	4	4	4	0	3	1	**4**	3	3	0	2	1	0	4
Intemperate family	9	4	5	8	11	10	3	7	2	3	**13**	7	2	7	1	4	9
Habitual drunkards	8	3	4	7	9	9	2	6	3	3	7	**11**	..	4	2	4	7
Temperate	3	0	1	2	1	2	1	1	0	0	2	..	**3**	3	0	0	3
Reformable	9	2	5	6	10	10	1	8	2	2	7	4	3	**11**	..	3	8
Hopeless	2	1	0	3	3	3	0	1	3	1	1	2	0	..	**3**	1	2
Have trade	5	2	4	3	5	5	2	6	2	0	4	4	0	3	1	**7**	..
No trade	11	2	4	9	11	12	1	6	3	4	9	7	3	8	2	..	**13**

TABLE IV.—ROBBERY.

Sane, 19—Neurotic Stock, 0—Total, 19.

	Sane.	Neurotic stock.	Orphans.	Not orphans.	Neglected childhood.	Habitual criminals.	First offenders.	Refuge boys.	Criminal family.	Pauper stock.	Intemperate family.	Habitual drunkards.	Temperate.	Reformable.	Hopeless.	Have trade.	No trade.
Orphans	12	..	**12**	..	7	10	2	3	2	3	4	5	2	6	4	2	10
Not orphans	7	..	..	**7**	2	7	0	2	2	1	6	4	1	2	4	0	7
Neglected childhood	9	..	7	2	**9**	9	0	5	2	1	5	6	1	5	3	2	7
Habitual criminals	17	..	10	7	9	**17**	..	5	4	3	10	5	2	7	7	2	15
First offenders	2	..	2	0	0	..	**2**	0	0	1	0	2	1	1	1	0	2
Refuge boys	5	..	3	2	5	5	0	**5**	1	1	4	4	1	3	2	2	3
Criminal family	4	..	2	2	2	4	0	1	**4**	0	3	2	0	1	2	1	3
Pauper stock	4	..	3	1	1	3	1	1	0	**4**	1	1	2	2	2	0	4
Intemperate family	10	..	4	6	5	10	0	4	3	1	**10**	5	1	4	5	1	9
Habitual drunkards	9	..	5	4	6	5	2	4	2	1	5	**9**	..	4	5	1	8
Temperate	3	..	2	1	1	2	1	1	0	2	1	..	**3**	3	0	0	3
Reformable	8	..	6	2	5	7	1	3	2	2	4	5	2	**8**	..	2	6
Hopeless	8	..	4	4	3	7	1	2	2	2	5	5	0	..	**8**	0	7
Have trade	2	..	2	0	2	2	0	2	1	0	1	1	0	2	0	**2**	..
No trade	17	..	10	7	7	15	2	3	3	4	9	8	3	6	7	..	**17**

4*   F

TABLE V.—FORGERY.

Sane, 11—Neurotic Stock, 3—Total, 14.

	Sane.	Neurotic stock.	Orphans.	Not orphans.	Neglected childhood.	Habitual criminals.	First offenders.	Refuge boys.	Criminal family.	Pauper stock.	Intemperate family.	Habitual drunkards.	Temperate.	Reformable.	Hopeless.	Have trade.	No trade.
Orphans	4	1	**5**	..	1	1	4	0	0	0	2	2	2	3	0	0	5
Not orphans	7	2	..	**9**	0	3	6	0	2	0	4	2	3	3	2	0	9
Neglected childhood	1	0	1	0	**1**	0	1	0	0	0	0	0	1	0	2	0	1
Habitual criminals	4	0	1	3	0	**4**	..	0	0	0	3	1	1	1	2	0	4
First offenders	7	3	4	6	1	..	**10**	0	2	0	3	3	4	5	0	0	10
Refuge boys	0	0	0	0	0	0	0	**0**	0	0	0	0	0	0	0	0	0
Criminal family	1	1	0	2	0	0	2	0	**2**	0	0	0	2	1	0	0	2
Pauper stock	0	0	0	0	0	0	0	0	0	**0**	0	0	0	0	0	0	0
Intemperate family	5	1	2	4	0	3	3	0	0	0	**6**	2	1	1	2	0	6
Habitual drunkards	2	2	2	2	0	1	3	0	0	0	2	**4**	..	2	0	0	4
Temperate	4	1	2	3	1	1	4	0	2	0	1	..	**5**	2	1	0	5
Reformable	4	2	3	3	0	1	5	0	1	0	1	2	2	**6**	0	0	6
Hopeless	2	0	0	0	0	2	0	0	0	0	0	0	0	0	**2**	0	..
Have trade	0	0	0	0	0	0	0	0	0	0	0	0	0	0	0	**0**	..
No trade	11	3	5	9	1	4	10	0	2	0	6	4	5	6	2	..	**14**

TABLE VI.—RECEIVING STOLEN GOODS.

Sane, 3—Neurotic Stock, 3—Total, 6.

	Sane.	Neurotic stock.	Orphans.	Not orphans.	Neglected childhood.	Habitual criminals.	First offenders.	Refuge boys.	Criminal family.	Pauper stock.	Intemperate family.	Habitual drunkards.	Temperate.	Reformable.	Hopeless.	Have trade.	No trade.
Orphans	0	2	**2**	..	2	2	0	0	0	1	1	1	..	0	2	0	2
Not orphans	3	1	..	**4**	0	3	1	1	0	1	2	0	..	3	..	1	3
Neglected childhood	0	2	2	0	**2**	2	..	1	0	0	1	1	..	2	2	1	4
Habitual criminals	2	3	2	3	2	**5**	..	1	0	2	2	1	..	2	0	0	4
First offenders	1	0	0	1	0	..	**1**	0	0	..	1	0	..	1	0	0	1
Refuge boys	1	0	0	1	0	1	0	**1**	0	..	1	0	0	1	0	1	0
Criminal family	0	0	0	0	0	0	0	0	**0**	2	..	..	..	..	..	..	..
Pauper stock	1	1	1	1	0	2	2	1	0	**2**	..	..	..	2	1	0	2
Intemperate family	2	1	1	2	1	2	1	1	0	0	**3**	1	..	2	1	1	2
Habitual drunkards	0	1	1	0	♦	1	0	0	0	0	0	**1**	1	..	0	1	0	1
Temperate	..	..	..	..	..	..	..	..	..	..	..	..		..	..	..	..
Reformable	3	0	0	3	0	2	1	1	0	1	2	0	..	**3**		1	2
Hopeless	0	2	2	..	2	2	0	0	0	1	1	1	..		**2**	0	2
Have trade	1	0	0	1	0	1	0	1	0	0	1	0	..	1	0	**1**	..
No trade	2	3	2	3	2	4	1	0	0	2	2	1	..	2	2	..	**5**

TABLE VII.—MURDER AND ATTEMPT TO KILL.

Sane, 14—*Neurotic Stock,* 6—*Total,* 20.

	Sane.	Neurotic stock.	Orphans.	Not orphans.	Neglected childhood.	Habitual criminals.	First offenders.	Refuge boys.	Criminal family.	Pauper stock.	Intemperate family.	Habitual drunkards.	Temperate.	Reformable.	Hopeless.	Have trade.	No trade.
Orphans	5	2	**7**	..	3	4	3	1	1	1	1	2	1	3	1	2	5
Not orphans	9	4	..	**13**	2	9	4	2	2	1	7	6	3	4	7	1	12
Neglected childhood	3	2	3	2	**5**	4	1	3	2	1	2	3	1	3	1	1	4
Habitual criminals	11	2	4	9	4	**13**	..	3	2	1	7	6	1	4	5	1	12
First offenders	3	4	3	4	1	..	**7**	0	1	1	1	2	3	3	3	2	5
Refuge boys	2	1	1	2	3	3	0	**3**	1	0	2	3	0	2	1	1	2
Criminal family	1	2	1	2	2	2	1	1	**3**	1	1	2	1	1	1	0	3
Pauper stock	1	1	1	1	1	1	1	0	1	**2**	1	0	1	..	1	0	2
Intemperate family	6	2	1	7	2	7	1	2	1	1	**8**	4	1	2	3	0	8
Habitual drunkards	6	2	2	6	3	6	2	3	2	0	4	**8**	..	3	4	2	6
Temperate	2	2	1	3	1	1	3	0	1	1	1	..	**4**	1	1	1	3
Reformable	4	3	3	4	3	4	3	2	1	..	2	3	1	**7**	3	0	8
Hopeless	4	4	1	7	1	5	3	1	1	1	3	4	1	..	**8**	0	8
Have trade	3	0	2	1	1	1	2	1	0	0	0	2	1	3	..	**3**	..
No trade	12	5	5	12	4	12	5	2	3	2	5	6	3	4	8	..	**17**

TABLE VIII.—RAPE AND ATTEMPTS, ETC.

Sane, 7—*Neurotic Stock,* 8—*Total,* 15.

	Sane.	Neurotic stock.	Orphans.	Not orphans.	Neglected childhood.	Habitual criminals.	First offenders.	Refuge boys.	Criminal family.	Pauper stock.	Intemperate family.	Habitual drunkards.	Temperate.	Reformable.	Hopeless.	Have trade.	No Trade.
Orphans	3	2	**5**	..	4	3	2	1	1	2	1	1	1	2	0	0	5
Not orphans	4	6	..	**10**	4	5	5	0	2	2	6	5	2	2	5	3	7
Neglected childhood	4	4	4	4	**8**	5	3	1	2	2	4	5	2	2	4	2	6
Habitual criminals	6	2	3	5	5	**8**	..	1	1	2	3	1	2	2	1	1	6
First offenders	1	6	2	5	3	..	**7**	0	1	2	3	1	1	1	0	0	6
Refuge boys	1	0	1	0	2	1	0	**1**	0	0	0	0	1	1	1	2	1
Criminal family	2	1	1	2	2	2	1	0	**3**	1	2	1	0	1	1	2	1
Pauper stock	1	3	1	2	3	2	2	0	2	**4**	1	1	1	0	3	1	3
Intemperate family	4	3	1	6	3	4	3	0	2	1	**7**	4	..	1	3	3	4
Habitual drunkards	4	2	1	5	2	5	1	0	1	0	4	**6**	..	3	4	2	2
Temperate	2	1	1	2	2	2	2	1	1	0	1	..	**3**	1	1	1	3
Reformable	2	2	2	2	2	2	2	1	1	0	1	1	1	**4**	..	1	3
Hopeless	3	2	0	5	2	4	1	0	1	3	3	3	1	1	**5**	1	4
Have trade	1	2	0	3	2	2	1	0	2	1	3	2	1	1	3	**3**	..
No trade	6	6	5	7	6	6	6	1	1	3	4	4	2	3	4	..	**12**

TABLE IX.—ARSON.

Sane, 4—*Neurotic Stock,* 3—*Total,* 7.

	Sane.	Neurotic stock.	Orphans.	Not orphans.	Neglected childhood.	Habitual criminals.	First offenders.	Refuge boys.	Criminal family.	Pauper stock.	Intemperate family.	Habitual drunkards.	Temperate.	Reformable.	Hopeless.	Have trade.	No trade.
Orphans	1	0	**1**	.	0	1	0	0	0	0	0	1	0	0	1	0	1
Not orphans	3	3	..	**6**	..	3	3	1	2	1	1	2	2	2	1	0	6
Neglected childhood	..	..	..	..		..											
Habitual criminals ..	3	1	1	3	..	**4**		.	1	2	.	2	1				
First offenders	1	2	0	3	..	..	**3**	.	1	2	1	2	1	.	2	.	4
Refuge boys	1	0	0	1	..	.	1	**1**	1	.	1	.	1	.	.		3
Criminal family	1	1	0	2	..	2	.	.	**2**	.	1	.	1	2			2
Pauper stock	1	0	0	1	..	1	.	1	.	**1**	1	.	1	.	1		1
Intemperate family..	1	0	0	1	..	1	.	1	.	.	**1**	1	1	.	1		1
Habitual drunkards .	3	0	1	2	..	2	1	.	.	1	.	**3**	.	2	.		3
Temperate	1	1	0	2	..	1	1	1	1	1	.	1	**2**	1	.		3
Reformable	..	2	0	2	..	.	2	1	2	.	1	.	**2**	2	.		2
Hopeless	2	1	1	2	..	2	1	.	.	1	.	2	.	.	**3**		3
Have trade	0	0	0	..													
No trade	3	4	1	6	..	4	3	1	2	1	1	3	2	2	3	.	**7**

TABLE X.—TOTAL CRIMES AGAINST PROPERTY.

Sane, 159—*Neurotic Stock,* 32—*Total,* 191.

	Sane.	Neurotic stock.	Orphans.	Not orphans.	Neglected childhood.	Habitual criminals.	First offenders.	Refuge boys.	Criminal family.	Pauper stock.	Intemperate family.	Habitual drunkards.	Temperate.	Reformable.	Hopeless.	Have trade.	No trade.
Orphans	74	8	**82**	....	46	67	15	19	11	23	33	33	16	36	26	15	67
Not orphans	85	24	..	**109**	50	84	24	29	21	22	50	41	16	46	34	26	82
Neglected childhood.	80	16	46	50	**96**	85	9	41	19	26	50	41	15	40	34	17	77
Habitual criminals ..	131	20	67	84	85	**151**	.	47	27	37	67	62	17	59	54	33	118
First offenders	27	12	15	24	9	..	**39**	1	5	8	16	12	15	23	6	8	30
Refuge boys	41	7	19	29	41	47	1	**48**	11	13	28	24	10	20	17	16	31
Criminal Family	23	9	11	21	19	27	5	11	**32**	7	15	11	4	14	9	7	24
Pauper stock	29	16	23	22	26	37	8	13	7	**46**	19	19	7	15	13	10	33
Intemperate family..	65	18	33	50	50	67	16	28	15	19	**83**	39	7	33	25	13	64
Habitual drunkards .	62	12	33	41	41	62	12	24	11	19	39	**74**	....	28	29	20	54
Temperate	28	4	16	16	15	17	15	10	4	7	7	....	**32**	18	6	4	26
Reformable	73	9	36	46	40	59	23	20	14	15	33	28	18	**82**	.	17	64
Hopeless	47	13	26	34	34	54	6	17	9	13	25	29	6	...	**60**	11	46
Have trade	30	11	15	26	17	33	8	16	7	10	13	20	4	17	11	**41**	....
No trade	128	21	67	82	77	118	30	31	24	33	64	54	26	64	46	...	**149**

TABLE XI.—MURDER, ETC., RAPE AND ARSON.

Sane, 25—*Neurotic Stock*, 17—*Total*, 42.

	Sane.	Neurotic stock.	Orphans.	Not orphans.	Neglected childhood.	Habitual criminals.	First offenders.	Refuge boys.	Criminal family.	Pauper stock.	Intemperate family.	Habitual drunkards.	Temperate.	Reformable.	Hopeless.	Have trade.	No trade.
Orphans...........	9	4	**13**	..	7	8	5	2	2	2	2	4	2	4	4	2	11
Not orphans........	16	13	..	**29**	6	17	12	3	6	5	14	13	7	9	12	4	25
Neglected childhood.	7	6	7	6	**13**	9	4	5	4	4	5	5	3	5	3	3	10
Habitual criminals..	20	5	8	17	9	**26**	..	5	6	3	13	13	4	6	11	3	23
First offenders	5	12	5	12	4	..	**17**	0	2	4	3	4	5	7	5	3	14
Refuge boys........	5	..	2	3	5	5	0	**5**	2	..	3	3	1	3	1	1	4
Criminal family.....	4	4	2	6	4	6	2	2	**8**	1	3	3	2	4	2	2	6
Pauper stock	3	4	2	5	4	3	4	..	1	**7**	2	2	2	0	5	1	4
Intemperate family..	11	5	2	14	5	13	3	3	3	2	**16**	8	2	3	6	3	13
Habitual drunkards.	13	4	4	13	5	13	4	3	3	2	8	**17**	..	5	9	4	12
Temperate	5	4	2	7	3	4	5	1	2	2	2	....	**9**	13	2	2	7
Reformable........	6	7	4	9	5	6	7	3	4	..	3	5	3	**13**	2	4	9
Hopeless	9	7	4	12	3	11	5	1	2	5	6	9	2	....	**16**	1	15
Have trade.........	4	2	2	4	3	3	3	1	2	1	3	4	2	4	1	**6**	..
No trade	21	15	11	25	10	22	14	4	6	4	13	12	7	9	15	..	**36**

TABLE XII.

CRIMES COMPARED BY PERCENTAGES.

	Total number of convicts.	Neurotic Stock.	Orphans.	Neglected childhood.	Habitual criminals.	Refuge boys.	Criminal family.	Pauper stock.	Intemperate family.	Habitual drunkards.	Without trade.
For all crimes	233	23.03	40.77	46.78	75.63	22.74	17.16	22.31	42.49	39.05	79.40
Crimes against person	42	40.47	30.95	30.95	59.52	11.90	19.04	16.66	38.08	40.47	85.71
Crimes against property............	191	16.75	42.93	50.26	79.05	25.13	16.75	23.50	43.45	38.74	78.01
Burglary..	48	18.75	39.58	58.33	83.33	31.24	20.83	33.33	33.33	33.33	81.25
Larceny, grand and petit..............	84	15.47	42.85	47.61	80.95	16.66	13.09	22.63	41.66	39.28	72.62
Larceny from person.	20	20.00	40.00	40.00	85.00	65.00	25.00	20.00	65.00	55.00	65.00
Robbery............	19	0.00	63.16	47.36	89.52	26.37	21.05	21.05	52.73	47.36	89.52
House of Refuge boys	53	15.09	45.28	88.67	98.15	......	24.52	24.52	50.96	50.96	60.38
Habitual criminals..	176	14.20	42.61	68.88	......	29.41	18.75	22.72	45.45	42.61	79.97

Table XII. gives the percentages on nine items contained in tables VI., VII., VIII., IX. and X., and to this is added a line for house-of-refuge boys. In statistics percentages are treacherous when the numbers on which they are computed are small, so that this table is given without claiming for it any great degree of authority, especially in the items of robbery and larceny from the person. But it is proximately reliable, because the elements out of which it is made were critically verified, because in the items of orphanage, neglected childhood, habitual criminals, refuge boys, criminal family, pauper stock, intemperate family, habitual drunkards, and without trade, the percentages ranging from one-fourth to three-fourths of the total enable an approximation to be made upon a very small number, even 50 unselected cases being sufficient in most of these items.

Nervously disordered stock.—Under this title are included all convicts who are or have been afflicted with insanity, epilepsy, idiocy, chorea, paralysis or other nervous disorder, or who have any blood relations who are or have been subject to any of these diseases. The number tabulated is greatly under the actual facts, because so many are either orphan or abandoned children who know nothing of their ancestry. Of the 233 prisoners examined, 49, or 23.03 per cent, belong to this stock, or nearly one in every four. If we compare the crimes against property with those of impulse, placing arson among that category as in table XI., we shall find that of the former there are 16.75 per cent of *neurotic* stock, while of the latter there are 40.47 per cent. This close relationship between nervous disorders and crime runs parallel with the experience of England, where "the ratio of insane to sane criminals is thirty-four times as great as the ratio of lunatics to the whole population of England ; or, if we take half the population to represent the adults which supply the convict prisons, we shall have the criminal lunatics in excess in the high proportion of seventeen to one."* In burglary we get 18.75 per cent and in larceny (grand and petit) we get a little under the average 15.47 per cent, while in robbery none are found. These ratios are not quite reliable, because those

* Dr. Wm. A. Guy, F.R.S. (Journal of Statistical Society, vol. xxxii. p. 16.)

who committed crimes against the person come from stocks who know their ancestry better than those who commit crimes against property, the orphanage of the former being 30.95 per cent or nearly one-third, of the latter 42.93 per cent or nearly one-half. It has been said that "whatever is physiologically right is morally right," * and here we have a confirmation of that saying by its converse, that whatever is physiologically unsound is morally rotten ; for we find that murder, rape and arson, crimes which arouse our abhorrence and indignation the most, for which the law awards the most severe penalties, and which all men in all nations are agreed to look upon as unpardonable, are perpetrated by a class of men whose probable capacity for self-government is twice and a-half less than that of criminals who prey upon property, and whose probable mental unsoundness, taking Dr. Guy's experience as the basis of calculation, is thirty-four times greater than that of the average community.

Inebriety.—Under the term "habitual drunkards" are included all such persons as get drunk at least once in three weeks, or whose passion for drink unfailingly induces them to intoxication whenever the opportunity presents itself, even if the intervals between debauches should be more than three weeks. It has been the aim of the investigation to establish if possible, the age at which inebriety was first begun, and the age at which the habit was fixed as an appetite. It was impracticable to make a discrimination between the occasional and the periodical drunkard, but other facts in the lives of those examined enable the construction of a series of four tables which illustrate the order of events in each career according to the plan of study set forth in "The Jukes !" †

In table XII. it will be found that 42.49 per cent of the total number of criminals are of intemperate family, while 39.05 per cent are habitual drunkards. With the house-of-refuge boys the ratios rise, respectively, to 51 per cent of intemperate family, and 51 per cent of habitual drunkards; but when we come to compare the habitual criminals to the first offenders we find that only 30 per cent of these latter belong to this class against 42.61 per cent of the

* Dr. Edmunds.   † See pages 39, 41.

TABLE XIII.—Habitual Drunkards, Showing Ancestry and Individual Characteristics.

SCHEDULE NUMBER.	Age at last conviction.	Venereal disease.	Prostitution, when begun.	INEBRIETY. Occasional, when begun.	INEBRIETY. Habitual, when fixed.	Intemperate family.	Mentally deranged or defective.	Neurotic heritage.	Criminal family.	Criminal type.	Trade or occupation.
75	28	? +†	?	16	20	?	No.	No.	Cousin	Habitual...	Moulder ?
5	31	?	?	17	18	F. habitual	Epil. in inf.			Habitual...	None.
61	42	?	No. ?	14	19	M. two genera'ns .	No.	Gra'mother palsy	No.	First offen'r	Painter.
136	23	?	?	15	20	?	No.	No	No.	First offa'r ?	None.
34	38	?	?	18	32	Father habitual..	No.	Aunt epileptic	No.	First offen'r	Puddler.
109	47	?	No. ?	10	25	Father habitual..	Insane 21	No		Habitual...	Canaller.
107	54	?	?	16	9	?	No.	Sister epileptic.		Habitual...	Tailor, 33 §.
72	35	?	?	16	20	Father habitual..	No.			Habitual...	Compositor ?
67	35	?	Yes.	19	25	F. habitual .	No.			Habitual...	None.
44	24	?	?	10	16	F. habitual .	No.			Habitual...	Canaller.
81	41	?	?	15	17	?	No.			Habitual...	None.
18	25	?	?	23	37	F. habitual .	No.			Habitual...	Laborer.
126	25	?	?	18	24	?	No.			Habitual...	Carpenter.
106	22	No.	?	16	17	F. occasional .	No.	No.	Uncle, cous.	Habitual...	Engineer.
56	17	G. 23 *	Yes.	15	22	Uncle habitual .	No.	Bro. epileptic.	No.	Habitual...	Book-keeper ?
27	40	No.	No...	16	16	?	No.			First offen'r	Messenger.
60	34	No.	?	17	20	?	No.	Bro. epileptic	No.	First offen'r	Jockey.
32	28	G. 20½	?	16	31	F. hab., M. occa'ly	Epileptic	Aunt insane		Habitual...	Plasterer.
3	21	No.	?	18	16	F. habitual .	No.				Broker's 'clerk.
61	19	No.	?	12	18	F. habitual .	No.			Habitual...	None.
44	42	No. ?	No. ?	10	17	?	No.			Habitual...	Peddling,
19	21		D. ||	7	18	?	No.	Mother paralysis.		Habitual...	None.
Average age...	31			14.69	24.52						

* The figures appended anywhere give the age.   § Learned in prison.   † An ? means unascertained fact or doubt as to the answer.
|| Declines to answer.

TABLE XIV.—HABITUAL DRUNKARDS, SHOWING ANCESTRY AND AGE AT WHICH VENEREAL DISEASE, PROSTITUTION AND INEBRIETY FIRST BEGAN.

Schedule Number.	Age at last conviction.	Venereal disease.	Prostitution, when begun.	Inebriety. Occasional, when begun.	Inebriety. Habitual, when fixed.	Intemperate family.	Mentally deranged or defective.	Neurotic heritage.	Criminal family.	Criminal type.	Trade or occupation.
40	*24	G. 21 ‖	16	20	23	F. habitual	No			First offen'r	Bricklayer?
57	*27	S. 18	14	20	22	F. habitual	No			Habitual	Sailor.
7	*28	S. 25 ‖	20	18	24	F. occasional	No		Bro. habit'al	Habitual	Laborer.
29	*22	S. 17	16	18	22	?	No		Bro. habit'al	Habitual	Laborer?
6	*33	S. 21	14	21	25	Father occasional	No	2 bros. idiotic, †		Habitual	Press work.
50	*26	G. 23	16	20	24	F. occasional	No			Habitual	Teaming.
4	17	S. 18	16	?	16	F. occasional	No		Brother	Habitual	None.
14	*22	S. 18	15	9	18	F. and bro. habit'l.	Weak mind.			Habitual	Bar-tender, 17.
84	20	G. 19	17	15	19	None	No		Bro. & cous.	Habitual	Teamster.
59	25	S. 18	17	12	21	?	No			Habitual	Clerk.
52	35	S. 20	17	18	25	F. habitual	No			Habitual	Soldier.
15	40	S. 31	20	18	30	F. habitual	No			Habitual	Baker.
86	*28	G. 16	13	9	18	F. habitual	No			Habitual	Sailor.
138	*23	S. 18	15	13	16	M. habitual	No		Bro. habit'al	Habitual	Shoemaker, §.
29	*18	S. 15½	15	14	16	Father occasional	Def. mind.			Habitual	Boot-black.
143	19	G. 19	15	14	Yes.	Father habitual	No.			Habitual	None.
35	27	G. 27	15½	8	Yes.	Mother habitual	Def. mind.			Habitual	None.
95	29	S. 18	16	12	Yes.	F. and bro. habit'l.	Insane, 28.	Bro. epileptic.	F. and bro.	Habitual	Cooper, 18 §.
22	42	S. 38	17	16	12	?	No.			Habitual	Cabinet-maker, §
89	*20	No.	10	16	19	None.	No.			Habitual	Moulder?
16	*28	?	15	18	28	None?	No.			Habitual	Steward?
84	*53	?	15½	20	16	F. hab., 2 bro. occ.	No.			Habitual	Laborer.
141	*37	?	17½	17	17	F. and 2 bro. hab'l.	No.	No.		Habitual	Tailor, §.
112	*23	?	16	16	20	F. and M. habitual	No.		Two bros.	Habitual	Candler.
83	*21	S.	18	18	18	F. and M. habitual	insane		F. & mother	Habitual	Lather.
70	25	?	15	17	Yes.		No.			Habitual	Laborer.
144	*24	?	15	16	22	F. occasional.	No.			First offen'r	Saloon-keeper.
90	20	?	13	15	17	F. occasional.	No.			Habitual	Butcher.
46	21	Yes.	14	13	Yes.	Cousin habitual	No.		Cousin	Habitual	Farm-laborer.
Average age.	26.42	20.84	15.60	15.13	21.56						

* Where prostitution precedes inebriety. † Aunt insane. § Learned in prison. ‖ G. stands for Gonorrhœa. S. for Syphilis.

¶ An ? means unascertained fact or doubt as to the answer.

TABLE XV.

CASIONAL DRUNKARDS, SHOWING ANCESTRY AND AGE AT WHICH VENEREAL DISEASE, PROSTITUTION AND INEBRIETY FIRST BEGAN.

SCHEDULE NUMBER.	Age at last conviction.	Venereal disease.	Prostitution, when begun.	INEBRIETY. Occasional, when begun.	INEBRIETY. Habitual when fixed.	Intemperate family.	Mentally deranged or defective.	Neurotic heritage.	Criminal family.	Criminal type.	Trade or occupation.
31	17	....	15	10	No....	F. hab, M. occas'l	No....	Uncle epileptic ...	Two uncles ...	First offen'r..	None.
129	24	....	16	14	No....	F. habitual	No....	....	Two bros....	Habitual ...	Brush-mkr, 14, §.
79	19	....	15	12	.....	....	No....	....	Bro......	Habitual ...	None.
94	22	....	22	19	No....	F. occasional	No....	....	....	Habitual ...	Farm-laborer.
1	*23	21	16	19	No....	....	No....	....	....	Habitual ...	Driver.
125	21	....	16	15	No....	F. habitual	No....	....	....	Habitual ...	Clerk.
41	17	....	15	12	.....	F. habitual	No....	....	Cousin	Habitual ...	Plasterer.
10	*22	....	15	17	.....	F. habitual	No....	2 aunts & gr' m. in.	....	First offen'r	Carpenter, 18.
24	24	....	18	17	.....	Father habitual	No....	....	No......	Habitual ...	Farmer.
Average age..	21	....	16.55	15.00	.....						

* Where prostitution precedes inebriety.   § Learned in prison.

TABLE XVI.

TEMPERATE, SHOWING ANCESTRY AND AGE AT WHICH VENEREAL DISEASE, PROSTITUTION AND INEBRIETY FIRST BEGAN.

SCHEDULE NUMBER.	Age at last conviction.	Venereal diseases.	Prostitution, when begun.	INEBRIETY. Occasional, when begun.	Habitual, when fixed.	Intemperate Family.	Mentally deranged or defective.	Neurotic heritage.	Criminal family.	Criminal type.	Trade or occupation
23	23	No	12	No	No	F. occasional	No	......	......	Habitual	Cook.
26	18	No	14	No	No	F. habitual	No	......	No	Habitual	None.
98	20	No	15	No	No	Parents temp.	No	......	No	First offender	None.
91	19	G. 18*	16	No	No	......	No	......	......	Habitual	None.
96	19	G. 22	22	No	No	......	No	......	No	First offender	Book-keeper.
29	28	S. ?†	17	No	No	......	No	Cousin epileptic	......	First offender	Clerk.
60	20	......	......	No	No	......	No	......	......	Habitual	None.
Average age..	21		16								

* G. means gonorrhœa.   † S. syphilis.   † An ? means unascertained fact or doubt as to the answer.

habitual criminals and 52 per cent of refuge boys. It must not, however, be argued from these figures that inebriety is *the* cause of these men becoming habitual criminals, because there are other causes of crime which, it is more than probable, are the common causes of both crime and intemperance, notably sexual excess and insane ancestry. To get at some indication of what are other elements, tables XIII., XIV., XV. and XVI. have been prepared.

Table XIII. gives habitual drunkards concerning whom the sexual habits have been unascertained and the venereal diseases are unknown or doubtful. Table XIV., gives habitual drunkards concerning whom the sexual habits have been learned. Table XV. gives occasional drunkards and Table XVI. temperate.

The average age at which the habitual drunkards began to drink is, according to Table XIII. 14.69 years and table XIV. 15.13, while the age at which the habit becomes fixed is (table XV.) 24.52 and (table XVI.) 21.56, or three years younger. In table XV., which tabulates the occasional drinkers, the average age when they begun is 15 years, but, on comparison of their average age at time of conviction, which is 21, we find it is below the average age at which the habit becomes fixed among the habitual drunkards (Tables XIII. and XIV.), which is 21.56 and 24.52 respectively, so that there is yet time for a portion of them to become habituals within the next three years and a half, which brings them to the average age when the habit was fixed as found in Table XIII. An examination of the rest of the table shows that there is less inebriety and nervous derangement in the ancestry of the occasionals, which may account for the age of fixed habits being retarded.

Coming down to particulars, we find that of 53 felons who are habitual drunkards, one began alcoholic indulgence at 6 years and is now insane ; one at 7, whose mother died of paralysis at 54 ; one at 8, whose mind is defective ; two at 9, one of whom is of weak mind, and four at 10, one of whom is now insane. Thus, out of nine boys, who began to drink at 10 years old or under, five of them are either insane, weak-minded, or the children of parents afflicted with brain disease. Of those who began to drink at 15 years or under, there are 25, of whom ten are either mentally deranged or the blood relations of those who have been thus affected, while of the 28 who have begun to drink at ages above 15, only five belong to that class. The age at which these 53 persons had the habit fixed was, one at 9 years old who is insane ; five at 16, one of whom is of defective mind ; five at 17, and six at 18, three of whom are insane or epileptic, and one whose mother died of paralysis ; while, of the twenty-nine who are 21 and under when the habit became fixed, eleven are either mentally deranged or belong to *neurotic* stock, and eleven are the children of habitual drunkards. Of the twenty-four who became habitual drunkards after they have reached their majority only four are afflicted with brain disease or belong to such families, and 7 are the children of habitual drunkards.

In the first three tables we find 6 cases where the mothers were intemperate. Of these four are mentally defective or deranged, the other two having blood relations who suffered from nervous disease. While the average age at which the total number began drinking is 14.72 years, that of these six is 12 years, and the average age at which the former became habituals is 23.04 years, of the latter it is 17.66 or five and one half years sooner. Whether these facts indicate that intemperance in the mother is more destructive than in the father, or that nervous disorders are a cause of inebriety or the reverse can hardly be decided by such meager facts. It is also noticeable that although the occasional drunkards and the temperate make an aggregate of 16, or nearly one-third as many as the habituals, not one of them is insane or nervously deranged ; while of the 53 habituals 8 are so affected.

On a comparison of tables XIII. and XIV., it appears that in the former, which contains a list of those inebriates with whom prostitution has not taken place at an early age, or who have declined to make any statement respecting this matter, we find that, while the average age at which they begin inebriety is six months earlier than in the other table, the average age at which they become habituals is 24.52, while in table XIV., where we find the average age at which prostitution begins is 15.60, the average at which habitual inebriety becomes fixed is 21.56, or three years younger. Nor is this all.

Out of thirty men in table XIV. seventeen of them have begun prostitution before or at the same time they have begun the habit of alcoholic indulgence, and the average age at which those who have contracted diseases resulting from sexual passion is actually below that at which they become habitual drunkards, the average age of infection being 20.84, that of habitual inebriety 21.56 — a difference of nearly nine months.

In the present stage of positive knowledge respecting inebriety, it would seem that, in a certain number of cases, intemperance is the cause of crime. "The best and most unprejudiced observers are agreed that the families of inebriates develop forms of nervous and brain diseases which could only be referred to the habits of drinking in the parent. Dr. Magnus Huss, of Stockholm, declared that drinking produced partial atrophy of the brain, which was handed down to the children. The brain was then too small for its bony case, and lunacy was the result. The same fact had been observed in the lunatics of Massachusetts. In France, Dr. Morel had observed the same result of diminished brains, through several generations, leading to imbecility, homicidal insanity, idiocy and final extinction." *

In another class of cases both inebriety and crime are the results of a common antecedent cause or causes; sometimes insanity or epilepsy in the parents, which, by transmission, changes its character to dipsomania; sometimes by physical exhaustion induced by starvation carried to a point that breaks down the constitution, or by habits of sexual debauch which create an appetite for alcoholism, or by other causes. What the specific cause may in each case be, must be determined if we wish to apply remedial measures, and the character of the remedy must differ with a difference in the initial, cause. With such inebriates as have acquired the habit, an appeal to reason, to tender memories and to self-respect may avail, because there may yet be will power left to affect a cure, when no such appeal will be of the least use where this failing is congenital, because it must be first and primarily treated

* *Alcoholic Ebriety.* Discourse by Elisha Harris, M. D., before the National Temperance Society, January 21, 1875.

as a medical question before it is approached as a moral one ; or rather, the moral treatment must be accomplished through the channel of physical cure as an antecedent and essential requisite.

Intermittent Industry. — Dr. Bruce Thomson, surgeon to the General Prison of Scotland, of eighteen years' experience, thus speaks of disease among criminals : " In all my experience I have never seen such an accumulation of morbid appearances as I witness in the *post mortem* examinations of the prisoners who die here. Scarcely one of them can be said to die of one disease, for almost every organ of the body is more or less diseased ; and the wonder to me is that life could have been supported in such a diseased frame. Their moral nature seems equally diseased with their physical frame ; and whilst their mode of life in prison reanimates their physical health, I doubt whether their minds are equally benefited, if improved at all. On a close acquaintance with criminals, of 18 years' standing, I consider that nine in ten are of inferior intellect, but that all are excessively cunning." *

These remarks, although substantially true of our own criminals, would present an overdrawn picture, and, after all, when we come to analyze cunning, it is a modified form of intellectual aptitude, the result of a very careful education of the faculties to escape detection, which training, had it been directed to other modes of gaining a living, would probably have produced the intelligence which Dr. Thomson here contrasts with cunning. Nor can the results of *post mortem* examinations be held to express the general physical condition of convicts, for those who die must necessarily be those in whom disease has worked its utmost ravages. But the substantial truth expressed in the foregoing statement makes the question one of the important branches of investigation, and one on which much of our treatment of the criminal class must depend if we propose to deal with the crime problem intelligently. Let us look to the effect of sickness upon the reputable classes. See how a bad cold, which " stops up the head," and brings with it ear-ache, stiff neck and sore throat, causes the most industrious man to lay up for a few days be-

* *The Hereditary Nature of Crime*, in Journal of Mental Science, vol. xv. p. 487.

cause he cannot work. How many of our merchants retire from business, preachers from their pulpits, lawyers from their offices, because ill health compels cessation from labor. Now, during the time these gentlemen are recuperating, away from their professional duties, be it one or more years, no one thinks of accusing them of laziness ; we justly call them invalids of different degrees. But when we cast our severe eye upon the criminal class, human beings who, in many cases, have inherited or acquired deep-seated constitutional diseases, we cease to reckon that disease with them will produce the same inability for continuous labor which we admit to be true among the worthy, and stigmatize their inaptitude for work as laziness. Now, the word laziness explains nothing. It merely describes a state which may be the result of any given twenty causes, or any combination of these, the true explanation becoming as complex a problem as human nature itself. But where we note the effect of physical and mental disease on the ability to work, we have at least one tangible and definite reason furnished to us for the laziness of the unbalanced, and we can then appreciate that certain congenital mental deficiencies and hereditary diseases have the effect of depriving the man of the power of sustained energy and account for those cases where " indolence is stronger than all the passions."

We find in table XII. that 79.40 per cent of the criminals examined have never learned a trade ; and while it is true that physical disease does not account for all the inaptitude of criminals, it does account for a great deal. As was said in the " Jukes," * one of the most conspicuous of the characteristics of the criminal is that, if he does work, he adopts some kind of intermittent industry which requires no special training. This view is sustained by the list of occupations on page 97.

* See " Jukes," p. 59.

True Trades Requiring Skill.

	Against property.	Against person.		Against property.	Against person.
Shoemaker	8	.....	Cabinet-maker	1	.. ...
Weaver	1	.....	Brush-maker	2	.....
Baker	1	.....	Confectioner	1	.....
Moulder	2	....	Plumber	2	.....
Wood-turner	1	.....	Blacksmith	2	.....
Tailor	3	.....	Photographer	1	.....
Wagon-maker	1	.....	Tinsmith	1	.. ...
Machinist	1	.....	Naval architect	1	......
Brass-finisher	1	.....	Carpenter	1	2
Jeweller	1	.....	Cooper	....	1
Umbrella-maker	1	.....	Puddler	....	1

True Trades Affected by Seasons.

	Against property.	Against person.		Against property.	Against person.
Plasterer *	1	1	Mate *	1	......
Stone Cutter *	1	.....	Engineer *	3	......
Painter *	4	.....			
Bricklayer *	1	.....	Total	50	7
Farmer *	7	2	Aggregate, all offenses		57

Occupations Requiring School Education.

	Against property.	Against person.		Against property.	Against person.
Compositor *	3	.....	Broker	1	. ....
Lawyer	....	1	Druggist	4	......
Actor *	1	......			
Bookkeeper	5	......	Total	21	3
Clerk	7	2			
			Aggregate, all offenses		24

Trades Requiring Slight Skill.

	Against property.	Against person.		Against property.	Against person.
Chair-caner	1	.....	Cook	1	......
Press-feeder *	6	.....	Barber	....	1
Spoke-finisher	1	.....	Butcher	2	......
Cigar-maker	1	.....			
Book-folder	1	.....	Total	14	1
Steward *	1	.....			
			Aggregate, all offenses		15

* The occupations marked with asterisks are classed as intermittent industries.

5   B

Occupations Requiring no Skill.

	Against property.	Against person.		Against property.	Against person.
Laborer *..	13	6	Sailor *	6	......
Newsboy *	2	......	Lather	1	......
Canaller *	4	3	Peddler *	1	......
Teamster *	7	2	Bar-tender	1	......
Boot-black *	1	......	Quack *	....	1
Messenger *	3	......	Fireman *	....	2
Waiter *	5	1	Brakesman *	....	1
Soldier *	1	......			
Farm laborer *	4	3	Total	52	21
Jockey *	3	2			
			Aggregate, all offenses		73

No Occupation.

Against property	55
Against person	9
Total	64

Recapitulation.

Total persons	233	Number requiring slight skill	15
Number of skiful mechanics	57	Number requiring no skill	73
Number requiring school education	24	Number who have no occupation	64

In a total of 233 persons, we find only 57, or 20.60 per cent, who have a trade which requires skill, 24 occupations requiring school education, 15 occupations that require but very slight skill, 73 requiring no skill, and 64 who have no occupation whatever. Of the total occupations, numbering 169, we find 113, or over 66 per cent, are of an essentially intermittent character, either by the interruption of the seasons, the daily exigencies of the weather, or the necessity of living away from home for longer or shorter periods. If we add the 64 who have no occupation, then we have 76 per cent who belong to the class who lack continuity of effort. But these figures do not express the true case ; for it does not follow that even those who have a trade have the perseverance to work steadily.

Without entering into an extended argument as to why the irregularity of diseased physical functions produces, at a second remove, irregularity in the voluntary efforts which we familiarly

---

* The occupations marked with asterisks are classed as intermittent industries.

call want of perseverance, we are justified by the highest medical authorities in saying that we thus get a series of social phenomena which are primarily physiological conditions. The physical disabilities which arrest the orderly growth of the body pròduce in the course of years a fitful character, partaking of the defects of the constitutional temperament which, because it is temperamental, dominates the habits of thought, of action and of sensation, and gives to the moral nature a vacillating form identical to its own spasmodic development. In this way the unfortunate victim unconsciously feels that continuous effort is the direction of greatest resistance, and falls into the position of a procrastinating and inefficient ne'er-do-weel if he escapes contaminating associations, or becomes an habitual criminal if he fall among thieves.

In discussing the importance and bearing of disease on the formation of industrial habits, the more remote causes and cure of criminal tendencies are being anticipated. Nor must the inference be drawn that, because it is of very great importance, it is the only cause for this defect of industrial aptitude ; there are two others of at least equal prominence. The first is one which is at the basis of all civilization, and without which it would be impossible ; it is that desire of the human race to secure the largest returns of enjoyment for the least expenditure of effort, and has led to the introduction of all the labor-saving machinery which so much multiplies our enjoyments. The other is education, which is capable of counteracting the effects of a defective physical organization, by correcting it through the formation of habits of regular application, which themselves react upon the vacillating temperament and contribute to the more healthy operation of the physical functions. We have here, then, three prime causes, which are so related to each other that we must reject the implication that, because a man has a defective physical organization, therefore he is necessarily irresponsible for his acts. That the insane are often irresponsible is true ; it is no less true that they commit criminal acts which are referrible only to physical disease ; but it is by no means true of the persons who are now under discussion.

Habitual criminals.—If we should rely upon the official figures to determine the ratio of habitual criminals, we should find they are set down at about 26 per cent, when an actual examination shows conclusively that the total for all crimes is 75.63 per cent; for crimes against person it is 59.52 per cent, and for those against property 79 per cent. Thus it turns out that in the crimes of design, which require training to insure success, and upon which the offender depends for his living, the proportion of habitual criminals is 19.48 per cent greater than in crimes of impulse.

With certain political economists, it has become customary to assert that crime does not pay. The main point relied on to sustain their view is that, on the average, the net booty obtained by crime is less than the average rate of wages, that criminals are subject to frequent imprisonment, and that they forfeit the advantages of the good opinion of their neighbors. All these positions are true if they were predicated of reputable people who are sensitive of their good name ; but they are not true when affirmed of habitual criminals. As to the good opinion of the righteous, that is a negative advantage which sinks to a level of absolute insignificance in the estimation of a clever pickpocket. The " habituals " have a community of their own ; they seek for the approbation of this circle and not that of the philanthropists and divines, whose code of propriety is incomprehensible to them and not unfrequently a subject of derision.

We must also dispossess ourselves of the idea that crime does not pay. In reality there are three classes with whom it does : 1st. The experts, who commit crimes which are difficult to detect or who can buy themselves off. These are the aristocrats of the profession. 2d. The incompetent, who are too lazy to work and too proud to beg, or too young for the poor-house. 3d. The pauper, who steals because prison fare and prison companionship offer higher inducements than poor-house fare or poor-house society. This stock amounts to 22.31 per cent of all criminals, as seen by table XII. The whole problem, so far as these three classes are concerned, resolves itself into the economic axiom of relative efficiency. The question with them is not : Does crime yield a rate of income less than that of a skilled mechanic ? But, does it yield a rate higher than any employer would be willing to pay for an inefficient, careless and untrained class such as the habitual criminals usually are? How incompetent they are for ordinary avocations of industry is seen when we find that 78 per cent of criminals in State prison are without trades, although their average age is 27 years, while only about 44 per cent are 20 years old and under, and none less than 16.

In the second place, some criminals make large fortunes, compound their felonies, and form examples of successful crime which allure the ambition of lesser rascals, just as the mercantile success of A. T. Stewart stimulates the ambition of a neophyte trader. It is quite true that they run the risks of imprisonment, but the average human mind is constituted to run risks. The miner, the engineer, the sailor risk their lives without hesitation for wages averaging from $15 to $150 a month and board; why should not the criminal be satisfied to run the lesser risks of his profession just as other men do in theirs. The question ceases to be: "Does crime pay on the average?" but "will it secure a prize in the lottery of chances?"

As the question presents points of practical use in the management and repression of the criminal class, aside from mere disputation, Table XVII. has been prepared, selecting 38 cases of habitual criminals, whose testimony on the questions at issue is deemed sufficiently trustworthy to be accepted as approximately correct.

From this table the average duration of criminal life of each habitual criminal amounts to 11.55 years, of which 7.84 are spent in criminal liberty and 3.71 in prison. Here we have a measure of crime risks which is far below the hazards of a miner, for, while he holds himself ready to spend 300 days, or 82 per cent of his life, in an occupation the conditions of which are far more onerous than that of imprisonment, and the remuneration of which yields not much above the bare necessaries of life, the criminal only gives up 34 per cent of his life to secure 66 per cent of license and self-indulgence. Furthermore, it appears that the average number of convictions in 12 years is 4.55, or one conviction in two years and six months. This accords with the estimate of one convict, that "there is from two to three years' average between commitments." For each commitment, the table shows an average of 146 offenses, and

TABLE XVII.

Showing Criminal Career, Offenses and Convictions.

SCHEDULE NUMBER.	Age at first offense.	Age at last conviction.	Total years of criminal life.	Total imprisonment to last conviction.	Net years of criminal liberty.	Total offenses.	Average number of offenses in one year.	Aggregate convictions.	Ratio of offenses to convictions.
6..................	7	21	14	2.0	12.0	M †	....	6	....
0..................	9	23	14	3.6	10.6	M	....	6	....
57.................	10	27	17	3.3	13.9	M	....	2	....
142................	9	19	10	1.6	8.6	M	....	3	....
119................	12	20	8	5.0	3.0	M	....	5	....
49.................	14	19	5	0.3	4.9	M	....	4	....
47.................	10	18	8	1.10	6.2	900	144	6	150 to 1
31.................	14	17	3	0.2	2.10	D ‡	....	2	....
120................	9	18	9	2.2	6.10	....	....	9	....
98.................	20	72	52	17.3	34.9	M	....	8	....
79.................	15	19	4	1.0	3.0	100	34	1	34 to 1
75.................	18	28	10	4.0	6.0	M	....	5	....
48.................	13	17	4	3.3	0.9	M	....	3	....
3..................	11	21	10	0.7	8.5	3,500	415	4	875.1
93.................	7	22	15	6.9	8.3	M	....	1	....
61.................	14	19	5	1.6	3.6	M	....	4	....
46.................	9	21	12	1.3	10.9	350	33	4	88.1
43.................	10	18	8	3.0	5.0	250	50	3	83.1
4..................	14	17	3	0.9	2.3	100	44	2	50.1
38.................	18	20	2	0.6	1.6	200	123	3	66.1
25.................	5	21	16	3.0	13.0	‖ 8?	§	5	....
86.................	9	22	13	11.0	2.0	10?	§	3	....
42.................	10	22	12	3.2	8.10	300	34	4	75.1
33.................	7	41	*34	10.3	23.9	5,000	218	16	317.4
0..................	9	54	*31	17.0	*14.0	M	....	8	....
78.................	14	19	5	1.3	3.9	M	....	4	....
70.................	14	25	11	6.9	4.3	M	....	8	....
62.................	13	27	14	3.0	11.0	M	....	8	....
129................	8	24	16	3.11	12.1	M	....	6	....
94.................	19	22	3	2.6	0.6	100	200	2	50.1
93.................	8	17	9	1.7	7.5	M	....	5	....
4..................	9	21	12	2.8	9.4	M	....	7	....
58.................	15	20	5	1.3	3.9	80	21	3	27.1
41.................	13	25	12	3.9	8.3	D	....	4	....
89.................	14	20	6	3.0	3.0	300	100	3	100.1
26.................	12	18	6	2.2	3.10	75	19	2	38.1
29.................	7	18	11	0.0	11.0	100?	9?	1	100.1
103................	9	19	10	4.2	5.10	....	....	5	....
Totals......	....	....	439	140.92	298.08	....	1,444	175	2,063 to 14
Averages ...	....	....	11.55	3.71	7.84	....	103	4.55	146 to 1

* Has been in insane asylums fourteen years of his life.   † M stands for "many offenses."
‡ D stands for "declines to answer."   § Rejected because grossly untrue.   ‖ Doubtful.

as about 100 offenses are committed each year, this would be equal
to one commitment for every 18 months of liberty, equivalent to 66
per cent of the total crime career. By adding 34 per cent, the
period of imprisonment, we get, as the time between convictions, by
this calculation, two years and three months, which again accords
with the statement of another convict, who testified that, for " small
crimes about 100 to 150 offenses to one conviction are committed, and
for big jobs, five offenses to one conviction ; but it takes sometimes
two years to put up a job on a bank." This computation would,
of course, not be correct for the total crimes committed in the
community, because this estimate refers only to State prison convicts.

It has been found impossible to get any reliable information as
to the average income of criminals from any calculation based
upon the value of the articles stolen as returned by the indictment,
for the tendency of the prosecutor is to enormously overestimate
the amount of his loss, and, in the second place, it is usually only
when a considerable loss has been sustained that the prosecutor is
roused sufficiently to give his time to secure the conviction of the
offender. For these reasons, $214, the average amount of each
theft which the schedules yield, is much above the actual truth as
respects the total criminal class, although it may be under the truth
for cases that receive State prison punishment, the higher crimes
being of course concentrated in this class of prisons.

To get a reasonable approximation of the net income, such prisoners as were sufficiently communicative were asked what yearly or
weekly income, by labor, they would think sufficient to restrain them
from theft. In most cases the question seemed so novel that they
were actually nonplussed. The habit of estimating expenditures
and of keeping in mind the relation between income and outgo was
so absolutely wanting, that they could form no approximate judgment on the question. The most consistent answers were : " One
thousand a year at shoemaking," providing he could work half the
time, " five hundred dollars a year ; " " seventy-five dollars a month,"
and " ten dollars a week," in most cases without any realization of
the value of money.

Reverting, at this point, to the testimony of a convict quoted

above, that those who do minor crimes commit about 100 to 150
offenses to *one commitment*, while those who " go for big money " get
caught once out of five times, we have here something which may
serve as a measure of police and public efficiency in preventing
crime.   Where large stores of valuables are kept, extra precautions
are taken by the owners ; where large sums are lost, the loser spares
no pains or expense to catch and punish the offender, and the
result is the convictions are 27 times more frequent in proportion to the number of offenses.   Nor is it fair to lay the chief blame
upon the police for not bringing petty offenders to justice more
frequently.   The blame is far more due to the public, which is so
careless or indifferent to its small losses, that it invites pilfering.   We
know of one person who nas lived 20 years of adult life and never had
his pocket picked, though a resident of the city for three-fourths of
that time, and another who has gone 40 years with a like experience,
while others get theirs picked, on an average, twice a year.   The
same caution in the latter case would, no doubt. produce the same
immunity as in the former, and would of itself go far to solve the
perplexing problem : What shall we do about our criminals ? One
answer is : *Lead them not into temptation.*

Relations of Crime and Pauperism.—In Table XII. it appears
that 22.31 per cent of State prison convicts are of pauper stock.
This is a considerable proportion, and it was intended to test whether the tentative inductions made in the " Jukes " * held good, that the
tendency of the oldest boy is to be the criminal, that of the youngest to be the pauper of the family ; but the inquiry was frustrated
from various causes and the material collected is not sufficiently
elaborated or consecutive to be available for record.   There are,
however, some facts which add to the evidence that the tentative
inductions there stated are correct.

" *Refuge* " *Boys.*—Under this title are included all boys who
have been sent to a reformatory, school ship, industrial school, or
house of refuge.   The total number of refuge boys is 53, or 22.74
per cent of the prisoners examined — the great mass of them being
city boys.   Dividing the total number of criminals into two cate-

* Inductions as to pauperism p. 38, § 10.—Inductions as to crime p. 47, § 4.

gories, those who are not refuge boys and those who are, we find that 68.88 per cent of the former are habitual criminals, while the latter rise to 98.15 per cent of their number. Thus, while the refuge boys furnish a little less than one-fourth of the prison population for all crimes, they yield 29.41 per cent of the total number of habitual criminals, or nearly one-third. It may be thought that the percentage of refuge boys is too great; but I have reason to think these numbers are below the reality, because to be a refuge boy is, among criminals, a term of reproach, and for this reason many of them deny having been inmates of a reformatory. In confirmation of this there are 11 cases scheduled whom it is most probable are house-of-refuge boys, but who have not been included in the tables as such because they are not *known* to be of that class.

Comparing crimes against property and person with each other, we find that while the first show 25.13 per cent of refuge boys or over one-fourth, the latter show only 11.90 per cent or about one-ninth of this class. Dismissing crimes against person and confining ourselves to crimes against property, we find that while they commit over 25 per cent of crimes against property, they commit 26.37 per cent of robbery, 31.24 per cent of burglary and 65 per cent of pocket-picking. Why do these boys commit crimes against property, and of these burglary and picking pockets by preference? In the first place it seems to be owing to the "congregate system," which allows abundant opportunity for criminal training. In a conversation growing out of the examination, one of them (see schedule No. 33, Table XVIII.) says : "I never learned a thing in my life in prison to benefit me outside. The house of refuge is the worst place a boy could be sent to." "Why so?" "Boys are worse than men; I believe boys know more mischief than men. In the house of refuge I learned to sneak-thief, shop-lift, pick pockets and open a lock." "How did you get the opportunity to learn all this?" "There's plenty of chance. They learn it from each other when at play." "But when you are at play you are otherwise occupied?" "Boys don't always want to play, and they sit off in a corner, and they get it" (criminal training). This man confessed to thirty arrests besides his sixteen convictions, and on the books of the prison is registered "second offense." Another boy, schedule number 25, after he had answered my questions, asked: "Please, sir, may I ask you a question?" "Certainly." "Why do they send boys to the house of refuge?" "I suppose it is to teach them to be better boys." "That's a great mistake, for they get worse." "How should that be?" "I wouldn't be here, only I was sent to the refuge." "What did you learn there that should have caused you to be sent here (Sing Sing)?" "I didn't know how to pick pockets before I went, and I didn't know no fences; that's where you sell what you steal, you know." "Yes, I know. How many fences did you learn of?" "Three." "What else did you learn in the way of thieving?" "I learned how to put up a job in burglary." During the cross-examination, when he was asked if he had learned a trade, he replied: "No, sir, only a branch of a trade." The answer was quite uncommon, so I asked why it happened. "That was in the refuge; they never learn you a trade; they learn you a branch of a trade, and keep you at it while you stay there." These statements may be exaggerations, but they certainly have great ground of probability. The fact is that the average refuge boy steals in the direction in which he is trained, and picking pockets and locks are the arts which can be taught in the reformatory with less chance of detection by the officers, than any others. In the 53 cases presented there is not one of forgery or false pretenses, for these require educational advantages which they do not get. It would be useful to know how much of the criminal recklessness which is found among refuge boys is owing to the imprisonment to which they are consigned at an early age becoming itself a training in cell life which effaces the wholesome dread of prison which the reputable youth universally entertain.

In Table XII. it will be found that 45.28 per cent of their number are orphans before their fifteenth year; 88.67 per cent are neglected children; 24.52 per cent are of criminal families; 24.52 per cent of pauper stock; 50.96 per cent of intemperate family, and 50.96 per cent habitual drunkards. With respect to the percentage of *neurotic* heritage, it must be borne in mind that a large

number of refuge boys are illegitimate, and do not know anything
about their paternity; for this reason it is impossible to get
reliable information as to the existence of nervous diseases in
their ancestry. Were this obtainable the percentage would undoubtedly be much higher than that shown in table XII., where it
appears as only 15.09 per cent. The average age at which their
childhood was neglected is 8 years and a quarter; they began crime
at 9 years and 8 months, 2 of them at 5 years, 4 at 7, and 5 at 8;
they went to the refuge at 12 years and 9 months, while their
present age is only 23. They began prostitution at the average of
14 years and 9 months, one beginning at 6 and one at 10, and had
contracted venereal disease at 19 years and 6 months, four of them
at 16 and under.

On taking a closer review we find 26 are habitual drunkards,
two of them before their ninth year, and of these 26 we know that
14 had parents who were habitual drunkards; 5 of these 14 are of
pauper stock, 6 are of criminal family, and 3 are either insane or of
nervously disordered stock. This statement does not exhaust the
story of the heredity; for out of these 26 habitual drunkards 4 had
occasional drunkards for fathers, while the ancestral habits of six
others are unknown; but it is to be remarked that not one has parents
recorded as temperate. Of the 21 who are occasional drunkards
only 2 have for parents habitual drunkards, while 2 have parents who
are temperate, leaving 8 whose parentage is unknown. It is also to
be remarked that of 16 criminals addicted to intemperance in any
degree who have parents known to be habitual drunkards, 7 belong
to criminal families, while the 37 other refuge boys show only 6
who are of criminal stock.

On inspection of Table XVIII., it will be seen that in 45 cases
out of 53 I was unable to get information as to the ancestral characteristics as to nervous disorders; otherwise the number would be
much greater.

Of the 8 who are of *neurotic* stock 3 are themselves deranged,
2 being insane in the asylum; 5 are habitual drunkards, one at 8,
one at 9, and one at 18, while 3 are known to be the children of
habitual drunkards, the ancestral habits of the other two being un-

TABLE XVII.

	Schedule Number	Offense	Ages — Neglected childhood	Ages — First offense	Ages — House of Refuge	Ages — Present	Imprisonment — Time sr. in refuge y.m.	No. impr'mnt	Ag. yr. of sentence y.m.	Habitual or 1st offendr	Criminal type — Whether of criminal stock	Licentious — In the stock	Licentious — When prost. begun
1	88	Burg. and lar.	9	9	9	27	.1	3?	6.?	H. §	....	....	
2	142	Burg........	7	9	10	22	2.0	3?	8.?	H.	Br. in H. R. ‡	....	Yes
3	38	Lar.........	....	? ¶	18	20½	.3	3	1.6	H.	....	....	No ?
4		P. lar......	9	9	14	60	5.0	8†	19.0	H.	....	....	
5	25	Lar.........	5	5	13	21	1.2	5	8.0	H.	....	M. Prost..	Yes
6	111	Lar.from pr..	12	12	No. ?	27	No.?	1?	4.5	H.	Br. & F. hab.	....	Yes
7	...	Burg........	5	9	9	30	.3	M*	11.6	H.	F. & M. hab.	....	6
8	3	Lar.from pr..	11	11	17	21	.6	4	5.7	H.	....	M. Prost..	
9	14	Att. to kill...	14	14	18	22	1.0	2	3.2?	H.	Bro. hab	....	16
10	4	Burg........	14	14	14	17½	.9	2	3.3	H.	....	....	16
11	138	Rob........	9	10	11	25	1.8	7	7.10	H.	....	....	13
12	86	Lar........	9	16	9	28½	1.0	3?	13.6	H.	....	....	16
13	40	L. from pr ..	Yes	No.?	No. ?	25	...	1	2.6	F o§	....	....	16
14	129	P. Lar	5	8	12	25	2.0	6	8.11	H.	2 br h. 1 br h r	....	16
15	26	L. from pr...	12	12	16	18	4.2	2	4.2	H.	....	....	14
16	61	Burg........	5	5	14	19½	1.6	4	4.0	H.	....	....	No ?
17	126	Rob. & burg.	10	....	12	27	.11	3?	6.6	H.	....	....	
18	80	P. Lar......	10	10	12	18	2.0	2?	7.3	H.	F. h. br. H.R	....	
19	140	Arson	Yes	17?	No. ?	17	....	1?	4.?	H.	F.& m.2 b.h r	....	
20	7	L. from pr...	9	....	13	28½	3.2	D†	3.2?	H.	....	....	20
21	143	Burg........	7	9	11½	20½	.8	3?	3.4	H.	....	....	13
22	74	Murder 1st ..	6	8	9	29	1.6	4	Life	H.	....	....	Yes
23	6	Robbery	6	7	10	28	.8	M.	17.0	H.	....	....	
24	33	Att. G. Lar..	5	7	8	41	3.6	16	12.9	H.	....	....	
25	153	L. from pr...	6	9	9	20	1.1	5	6.8	H.	....	M. Prost..	16
26	141	Robbery	12	....	14	21½	1.10	2?	3.10	H.	....	M. Prost.	17½
27	89	L. from pr. .	10	....	14	20	1.1	3	4.0	H.	....	....	10
28	128	Att. to kill...	11	....	11	24	1.0	3	21.6	H.	....	....	
29	4	Lar........	8	9	9	19	4.0	7	5.8	H.	....	....	Yes
30	42	Lar........	10	10	15	19	1.8	4?	5.8	H.	....	....	14
31	54	Robbery	6	7	10	21½	6.0	5	13.6	H.	Bro. H. R...	M. Prost..	18
32	58	L. from pr...	15	15½	17	21	.9	3	3.9	H.	....	....	18
33	41	L. from pr...	12	....	13	25	.9	4	4.9	H.	Bro...	....	14
34	91	Burg	9	9	14	24	.9	4	11.0	H.	....	2 sist. prost	Yes
35	127	L. from pr. .	10	....	12	19	1.0	2?	4.0	H.	Bro. H. R...	....	
36	131	R. stolen gds.	12	....	13	23	.6	2	4.6	F o?	....	....	
37	119	Burg	6	....	13	20	3.7	5	8.0	H.	....	M. Prost.	
38	145	G. Lar	12	....	12	24	2.3	3?	8.3	H.	....	M. Prost..	No ?
39	93	Burg	7	7	14	22	1.9	5	11.3	H.	....	M. Prost..	No ?
40	43	Burg........	10	10	13	18½	1.6	3	5.0	H.	....	....	15
41	47	Burg........	10	10	12	19	2.10	6	4.4	H.	....	....	13
42	93	P. L. from pr.	5	8	8	19	1.7	5	6.7	H.	1 Bro. hab.	....	Yes
43	31	Burg........	17	....	Yes	31	....	2?	3.2	H.	....	M. Prost..	
44	120	L. from pr...	7	....	9	19	1.7	9	5.6	H.	....	M. Prost..	
45	76	L. from pr...	7	9	9	23	.1	2?	2.6	H.	Bro. hab. ..	....	16
46	51	Lar........	7	6	18	23	1.6	5	5.10	H.	....	....	
47	78	P. Lar......	4	....	15	20	1.0	5	2.0	H.	M. bro. H. R.	M. & s. pro	....
48	56	Att. Rape...	9	....	10	19	3.0	2	4.3	H.	....	....	
49	48	Burg........	6	8	13	18	3.4	3	5.0	H.	....	....	
50	139	Lar	....	....	....	26	‖		1 o?		....	....	
51	121	Burg........	....	....	....	19	....		2.?	H.	....	....	
52	91	Burg	10	13	15	18½	.9	4	3.3	H.	....	....	16
53	130	Lar.	11	11	14	21	3.0	2?	7.11	H.	No ?........	....	....
		Average age	8.27	9.61	12.21	23.02	1.6						14.77

Explanations.—† Declines to answer. ‖ 5 days. * Many times. ¶ Doubtful. ‡ H. R. House.
F. O. First Offender. †† Vag. Vagrant. ‡‡ O. R. Out Door Relief. ¶¶ Learned in Prison or Refuge.

—Refuge Boys.

Age when venerial disc. first appear'd.	Age begun.	Habitual drunk'rd.	Character of family.	In the individual.	In the stock.	Father dead.	Mother dead.	Individual, what form.	In the stock.	Trade or occupation.
	ness.	Inebriety.		Nervous diseases.		Orphan-age.		Pauperism.		
	Indv'ual.		Family.							
......	No	....	....	No	Bro. ep..	No	10	......	....	Plumber.
......	Yes	....	....	No	F. ep....	12	16	No...	M. & s. O. R.	Shoes, ¶¶
......	Yes	....	F. hab.....	....	Bro. ep..	No	No	......	....	Teamster.
......	6	9	....	in.21	....	No	No	Vag†¡	....	Tailor 23, ¶¶
......	7	8	....	No	M. Para.	0	No	......	....	None.
......	12	Yes	F. hab.....	No	1 b.in. 1 ep	No	No	No...	....	Machinist.
S **	10	Yes	F. & M. hab.	In.	....	No	No	P.h.1c	M.& s.p.h.§§	Laborer.
**G20½	16	18	M. occ. F. h.	Ep..	Aunt in.	10	No	......	M.—O. R...	None.
S. 18	9	18	F. & bro. h..	No .	....	No	No	No...	....	Bar-tender.
S. 16	16	Yes	F. hab.....	No .	....	No	No	No...	Mother	None.
S. 18	13	22	F. hab.....	No .	....	No	No	......	....	Shoe, ¶¶
G. 16	9	18	F. hab.....	No .	....	No	No	......	....	Sailor.
G. 21	20	23	F. hab.....	No .	....	2	No	No...	....	Bricklayer, ?
......	14	Yes	F. hab.....	No .	....	No	No	No...	....	Brush-mk.¶¶
No	No?	No?	F. hab.....	No .	....	No	No	No...	....	None.
No	12	17	F. hab.....	No .	....	No	No	......	....	Gasfitting.
......	16	17	F. hab.....	No .	....	No	11	......	B. & s. o. asy.	Engineer.
......	....	Yes	F. hab.....	No .	....	No	No	Vag..	F. vag......	B'sh-mkig,¶¶
......	No?	No?	F. hab.....	No .	....	No	No	......	....	
S. 15	20	24	F. occ.....	No .	....	No	No	No..	Parents O. R.	Laborer.
G. 25½	12	Yes	F. occ.....	No .	....	No	No	No...	....	
......	16	Yes	F. occ.....	No .	....	No	No	No...	....	
......	14	Yes	F. occ.....	No .	....	No	No	......	....	L'ngsho'man.
S. 31?	....	29	....	No .	....	No	No	......	....	Shoes, ¶¶
......	....	Yes	....	No .	....	5	No	......	....	Teamster.
......	17	19	....	No .	....	4	1	......	....	Tailor, ¶¶?
No	18	19	....	No .	....	No	No	No...	M. O. R....	Brass-m'lder.
......	19	Yes	....	No .	....	11	No	No. .	....	Carpenter.
......	....	Yes	....	No .	....	No	5	......	....	Ca'ingchrs ¶¶
S. 16	Yes	No	7 unc. h.,F. o.	No .	....	No	No	......	....	Actor.
......	Yes	No	M. hab.....	No .	....	0	No	Vag..	....	Shoes, ¶¶
G. 18	Yes	No	F. occ	No .	....	No	15	......	....	Plumbing.
G. 21	Yes	No	F. occ.....	No .	....	5	No	No...	....	Compositor.
S. 18	Yes	No	F. & m. occ.	No .	....	No	No	No...	....	Machinist.
......	15	No	F. occ......	No .	....	No	No	......	O. R. 3 years	None.
......	Yes	No	F. occ......	No .	....	No	No	......	....	Shoes, ¶¶
......	14	No	M. occ......	No .	....	0	No	o. r.13	....	None?
......	Yes	No	F. occ.....	No .	....	No	No	......	....	Jockey.
No	Yes	....	....	No .	....	?	3	......	....	None.
......	Yes	....	....	No .	....	7	12	......	....	None.
......	Yes	No	....	No .	....	3	10	......	....	None ?
......	Yes	....	....	No .	....	No	No	......	....	None ?
......	Yes	No	....	No .	....	0	No	......	....	Laborer.
......	12	No	....	No .	....	No	No	......	....	
S. 20	Yes	No	Temperate ..	No .	....	No	No	......	....	Blacksmith.
......	Yes	....	Temperate ..	No .	....	No	No	......	....	Laborer.
......	No?	No	M. occ......	No .	....	1	No	O. r.‡‡	M. & s. O. R.	None ?
......	No	No	....	No .	....	No	5	No...	....	None ?
.... .	No	No	....	No .	....	No	No	......	....	Shoe, ¶¶
......	No	No	....	No .	....	No	No	No...	....	Shoemaking
.....	No	No.	....	No .	....	....	....	......	....	None.
No	No	No	Par. temp...	No .	....	No	No	No...	....	None.
......	No	No	F. temp.....	No .	....	No	No	......	....	None ?

19.57 | .... | ....

known, one of them however having a mother who died of paralysis; 3 of these 5 habitual drunkards are of pauper stock, while 2 of them had prostitute mothers, 2 others are of criminal stock, the parentage of the other being unknown. It thus appears that the *neurotic* House of Refuge stock shows a cumulation of misfortune both as to heredity and environment which accounts abundantly why they are incurable criminals.

Typical classes of criminals.—The large proportion of habitual criminals raises the question : How shall their number be de' creased ? This requires the citing of typical cases which suggest reflections on the manner in which the law and the prison now deal with them.

1. Of those who are essentially not criminal, who are of sound mind and body, honest and industrious and of good stock, there are, among State prison convicts, from 1 to 2 per cent. They are usually committed for crimes against the person, and belong to that class of men who are benefited by imprisonment, if the term of sentence is not too long. What they need is protection from the after recognition of habitual criminals, from contamination by loss of self-respect, and opportunity for mental culture.

2. First offenders who fall because they are vain, self-indulgent, and in the toils of lewd women. They abuse trusts by embezzlement, and represent a class who are quite too numerous in our midst. When detected they often escape prosecution altogether for the sake of their parents, and because they are personally liked. The type is that of a descending family, in which the misuse of good faculties and the abuse of opportunities conspire to lead astray, but the good teachings of youth and the dear associations of home make reformation easy.

3. First offenders who have been led off into crime by bad associates. They are children of honest parents who, from indulgence or want of capacity, have not brought them up judiciously.

In the foregoing we have what may be called types of sporadic crime, in which the primary element of disorder is only a movement of momentary passion kindled partly by feelings of self-respect, or educational neglect, uncomplicated by insane or **criminal heredit-**

ary tendencies, and in which the criminal habit has not become fixed.

4. Convicts of low vitality, born of pauper parents, who have left them orphans in childhood so that they have drifted into habitual crime.

5. Illegitimate children born of intemperate, vicious and criminal parents, who have trained them to crime.

These types have, in addition to parental neglect, a hereditary tendency to crime, pauperism or premature death. Many are, however, reformable, and, if such treatment is to be applied, the prerequisite is a knowledge of the ancestral defects, because the heredity is the main factor in their lives.

6. Contrivers of crime who look upon crime as a legitimate business, who "don't do no light things," but "go in for big money," and are irreclaimable.

7. Active executors of crime, who have past their thirty-fifth year and are casting about to abandon the field as executors of crimes, to enter that of crime capitalists.

8. Panders to the vices of criminals, themselves the active abettors in facilitating crime.

In this series, whatever may have been the road which each has travelled, whether forecast by hereditary transmission or induced by miseducated childhood, these men, past reform, dangerous and desperate, are of service to the State only as examples of the austerity of her justice.

9. Men who have acquired epilepsy or insanity, and whose crimes are, probably, the results of perverted minds.

10. Unfortunates who have inherited nervous and brain diseases which destroy the moral sense.

11. Persons who have forms of nervous disease which destroy the will power over the voluntary motions, and do acts of impulse which result in murders, attempts to kill and rape.

Methods of Treating the Unbalanced.—In whatever form or degree crime takes place, it is an indication of want of balance produced by some kind of disability which needs a treatment appropriate to the conditions producing it. There are two modes of dealing with the crime problem, the immediate or correctional, which acts upon the individual offender quickly and relates more specially to the administration of the law, the efficiency of the police, the perfection of prison discipline ; and the remote or preventative, which requires long periods of time to mature, and anticipates the development of the potential offender by effecting ameliorations in public health and general education, which remove the causes of crime.

The Immediate or Correctional Method.—In the State of New York we have seven separate classes of penal and correctional institutions for the detention of accused persons and the punishment of different degrees of crime committed at different ages. These are Juvenile Asylums' for truant and vicious children, Reformatories for youths under 16 years who have committed crime, Police lock-ups for temporary detentions, Workhouses for misdemeanors, County jails for minor offenses, Penitentiaries for crimes not of the highest degree and for certain classes of felons who are yet young, and State Prisons for crimes of the highest degrees. In all these penal institutions, until recently, the only correctional method employed was that of the Congregate System of imprisonment, which, bad at first, has, in the State prisons in half a century, degenerated by progressive and successive forms, kinds and degrees of official corruption, ignorance and perhaps still more dangerous indifference, until it has neither philosophy, ascertained experience, justice, public advantage, or common sense to recommend it.

In the foregoing statement of typical classes of criminals we have an enumeration of different fundamental crime causes, which range under a few general heads. Some men do not learn right from wrong because the physiological quality is poor ; some because the balance between passion and judgment is so ill adjusted that they run into excesses ; some from nurture in crime ; others from educational neglects. It is from a discriminating consideration of these and of allied facts, in each individual case, that the possibility of reform can be determined, and where they are accurately measured, the limits of such reform can be established. Where the defect is congenital, as in idiocy, our power to control it is least ; where functional, as in the earlier stages of insanity and other diseases, it is greater ; where it results from educational neglect, it is greatest. But no scheme which has but one method of dealing with every class of cases, can be of any general value. Is there not more in human nature than in any human device which does not include all varieties of human aberration and adapt itself to their multiplex requirements ? To meet the exigencies of the problem the State of New York has hitherto provided a prison, ranged the perhaps epileptic felon in a gang to learn the lock step to torment the shattered nerves, the fragment of a trade that supplies the murderous or suicidal weapon, the congregate idleness that prepares for solitary debauch, the enforced companionship of felons in the stratified dormitories, where unmentionable crimes are perpetrated —inevitably perpetrated, because of the predisposing sloth—till, at last, the exhausted brain breaks down, and the congregate system adds one more maniac to the long list of wrecked lives which its many deficiencies create, or returns the felon upon the community a more dangerous offender.

What is wanted is that an order and kind of treatment in accordance with the ascertained deficiencies of each person shall be the key of the method of training, adopting any passion or emotion which is yet sound or serviceable for the purpose as a point of departure in the new education, and a weapon to conquer or amend the frailties of the character, thus making any good trait the nucleus for the crystallization of better habits.

In the " Jukes " it was shown that heredity depends upon the permanence of the environment,* and that a change in the environment may produce an entire change in the career, which, in the course of greater or less length of time, according to varying circumstances, will produce an actual change in the character of the individual.† Now, if the environment furnishes the elements of the mental nutrition, and largely determines by that means the character of the mental and moral growth, what are we to think of a prison system which, with vast perfunctory incompetence, masses an army of moral cripples, cursed with contaminating characteristics

* See proposition 5, page 66. † The " Jukes," 58.

H

held in common, and thus, under the imposing title of " the congregate system," prepares an environment of criminal example just
fitted for the assimilative power of each individual malefactor?
Upon what grounds shall we continue this system when the experience of other nations has demonstrated that *three years* of separate
imprisonment has more effect in checking crime than *ten years* of
congregate custody ; that it reduces the necessity of punishment ;
that it prevents the contamination of the reformable ; that it pro-
tects the convicts from recognition by their co-prisoners when
liberated ; that it checks the formation of gangs for future criminal
operations, and that it cuts off the possibility of odious crimes
which rivet the criminal habit because they obliterate the sense of
self-respect and the voice of conscience as the first step in a mental
degeneration that ends in a maniac's demise.

The best experience as respects all institutions is against the
aggregation of similar defects, or similar misfortunes within the
walls of a spacious building. The large hospital is making way
for the pavilion, and in many cases the tent in the open air with its
single patient ; the orphan home, for the domesticating of the child
in private families ; the foundling hospital, for the nursing-out
system ; and the insane asylum, for the private treatment of the
mentally deranged. It is useless to resist a tide which thus sweeps
from all directions, and must necessarily carry away the congregate
method of treating every form of human infirmity.

Fortunately for our State, the recent adoption of a constitutional
amendment abolishing the political mismanagement of our State
prisons and the establishment of the Elmira Reformatory have
already produced reforms in the law and the administration of
penal discipline which give great promise.

As respects the amendment of the criminal law much needs to
be done, but there is room here for only two features, relating
to irreclaimable criminals and epileptics.

In dealing with the typical habitual criminals who are contrivers
of crime, criminal capitalists and panders, where we cannot accomplish individual cure we must organize extinction of their race. They
must sternly be cut off from perpetuating a noisome progeny either

by the propagation or perversion of a coming generation. The old laws attempted this extinction by hanging ; but for us it must be perpetual imprisonment, with certain mitigations to guard against barbarity. For this class, congregate imprisonment is perhaps the most suitable.

In discussing the question of homicidal tendency among a certain class of epileptics Dr. Maudsley says : " The attack of homicidal mania may take the place of the ordinary epileptic convulsions ; being truly a *masked* epilepsy. The diseased action has been transferred from one nervous centre to another, and instead of a convulsion of the muscles the patient is seized with a convulsion of ideas. * * * These are facts of medical observation—first, that an outbreak of irresistible homicidal impulse may occur in a person who has the epileptic *neurosis*, without there ever having been an attack of actual epilepsy ; * * Secondly, that it may immediately precede or really take the place of an attack of epilepsy in either of its forms ; and thirdly, that it may follow an attack of epilepsy * * * ' sudden and irresistible impulses being,' as Trousseau remarks, ' of usual occurrence after an attack of *petit mal*, and pretty frequent after a regular convulsive fit.' " *

The following is a case in point :

T. C——d, aged 47 ; assault and battery ; six months in penitentiary. Is of a sanguine, lymphatic temperament, average vitality, good general health, but apathetic. He is intelligent, with a fair stock of useful knowledge, and was a school teacher when young, but now is an upholsterer. His moral sense is fair, but his will is weak. He served in the rebellion for nine months and was wounded in the head by a ball, which fractured the skull ; was insensible for several months, and after being trepanned came back to consciousness ; in 1864 had an epileptic attack, a consequence of the injury received by the brain, and in the last 10 years has had ten or twelve epileptic seizures. Has probably been committed before for similar offenses ; confesses that he has been in brawls before, and that, when he gets a little liquor, he " gets off his head." Says he can't drink much for it makes him wild. This, while somewhat exagger-

* *Responsibility in Mental Disease*, by H. Maudsley, M. D., pp. 166, 169.

ated, is quite consistent with his acquired epilepsy. In the upper posterior portion of the head, on the right side, is a depression of the skull from the bullet wound, in which the first joint of the finger may be laid to one-third its thickness. What this man needs is to be withdrawn from the temptation of drink and placed where he will not be excited. There is hardly a doubt that he will commit murder some day ; not because he is of a vicious or malignant temper, for his disposition is mild and apathetic, but because his epilepsy may at any moment be developed into a homicidal impulse which he cannot control. This man will probably be returned again and again to prison on short sentences for acts which are the direct result of disease, which will never be checked on account of the deterrent effect of imprisonment, and will cost the State heavily for continual arrests and trials. Will presiding justice in our courts of law ever put her finger into that wound and learn what is the matter with this man ? Yes, most undoubtedly, *when he has murdered some poor victim in some shocking way*, then she will say that he must not be hanged because he is irresponsible. When justice does put her hand upon that wound she will have to call a physician to guide it to the spot ; for is not justice blindfold ? And it will not be justice either which decides whether the man is responsible for his violence or not, but it will be the doctor's dictum. Why should justice neglect to keep the doctor by, to help her to a wise judgment of his case when he is summoned at her bar for assault and battery, and make a fitting disposition that will forestall his braining a human creature ? This is no improbable case : it has frequently occurred. Three years ago an epileptic was committed to Sing Sing. Shortly after, he was transferred to the insane asylum and discharged from thence when his term expired. Within the last eight months he has again passed through the courts, been recommitted to Sing Sing, and one month ago was seized with an epileptic fit during which time he killed a fellow-convict, after which he was again committed to the insane asylum, this time probably for life. Justice being blind, why should she neglect to make a medical inquest whenever an attempt on life has been committed, and, where the evidence shows such dangerous brain disorder, commit the accused to an insane asylum for life? In the case of an attempt to kill, in what respect does it differ from murder, except in the fact of being not fatal?

The Remote or Preventive Method.—In this aspect the study of criminal careers merges into a larger inquiry than its own special domain, and for its complete solution embraces the whole science of life. From this point of view, the analysis of crime causes includes all the physiological and social phenomena which affect the well-being and stability of the race, in which the combined forces of the Court of General Sessions and the policeman's club play but a minor part. The fact that our present civilization is a growth through countless generations,—the result of constant and cumulative training,—seems to indicate that a discovery of the method and order of this growth, applied as a method of education, would develop, in a few generations, and in exceptional instances in a single individual, a mental and physical condition approximating that which it has taken countless generations to evolve. That this process is now measurably understood, makes it possible to adapt it to the reform of the criminal class.

In discussing the question of intermittent industry, it was shown that one of the causes of idle habits was, primarily, physical and mental disease. Now, a large part of the disease which prostrates the community is entirely controllable by sanitary precautions. The first condition, therefore, of social and moral regeneration is public health. The draining of lands, the sewerage of cities, the ventilation of houses, the amelioration of tenements, the cleansing of streets, the widening of thoroughfares, the demolition of rear buildings, the removal of cesspools, the purity of water supplies, the abundance of fresh air, are only a few of the conditions which, if observed, will so improve the health of the general community that they will be more capable, and for that reason more willing, to do their work without exhaustion than they now are. With this increment of vitality they will need less and, therefore, consume less of inebriating stimulants than they now do. Public health will react against intemperance in all its forms, and this again will react in maintaining and perfecting public health. In a community in which its infants are blessed with the advantages of perfect hygienic training, the body will assume that steady, uninterrupted growth which is the first requisite for the organization of a sound mind and its concomitant — a well-balanced life. Then will be possible the next great step in the larger domain of crime cure, the educational question. Those who comprehend the specific process of moral education, that it begins with certain concrete acts which, by repetition and variation, organize in the mind definite and permanent abstract conceptions of right and wrong, will see at once that the foundations of the moral character must be laid in the earliest infancy and must begin by the education of the senses. From babyhood, infants must have liberty to use their limbs, toys to occupy their attention when awake, and when they are able to walk, their play must be so directed that, at least a portion of it, shall take a systematic form which produces objects of beauty or of use as permanent results of their manual dexterity. Various materials, such as those suggested by Froebel in his Kindergarten education, must be given to the child to be fashioned into multiform objects so that knowledge will be gained by the use of the hands and eyes. This exercise of the hands forms the basis of industrial training and unconsciously organizes the habit of industry, so that it becomes not only of easy performance but an essentially necessary activity of the waking hours. Given a taste for steady work and you have the best possible safeguard against the unbridled indulgence of the passions, and with this, an effectual check to the formation of criminal practices which are, in a majority of instances, the direct result of indulgence in exhausting vices, or in the feverish pursuit of indulgence which a hard-working man does not think of and for which thefts and embezzlements are committed. But the industrial training here advocated must not be the arbitrary imposition of a formal task. Work is not an education, in its proper sense, unless it enlists the putting forth of the powers of body and mind, simultaneously and cheerfully, to accomplish a predetermined result. For this reason, the "team system" of industry for children and youths, which is almost universal in our houses of refuge, is an educational blunder, and not industrial training in its proper sense. It does not produce habits of industry because it fails to employ the mind, and as the fraction of a trade it teaches soon becomes a purely automatic operation that requires no attention, the mind is left free to rove over the recollections of vice and schemes of mischief, which it is the purpose of the reformatory to obliterate by training.

Thus public health and infant education conforming, in general plan, to Froebel's Kindergarten school, are the two legs upon which the general morality of the future must travel. It may be objected that the general community is not sufficiently trained to understand and to establish rational education as here indicated. If this be so, it is at least possible to order that a few hundred of the large number of the orphans supported by the State shall be dealt with according to the most approved methods of education. In St. Louis, Missouri, the Kindergarten education has been introduced in the public schools, and observers of its effects say that it has a marked tendency to prevent hysteria among girls. If this is true, how important an auxiliary must it be to a class of human beings who are, according to Bruce Thomson, seventeen times more liable to nervous disorders than the average community !

In the preceding pages I have endeavored to show that the two great factors in a well-balanced life are a healthy body, properly developed, and a sound and broad judgment, resulting in a well-fashioned and powerful will. It now only remains to add that the same methods which will secure the advantages of these for the general community, will also be efficacious when applied to the rectification of unbalanced lives. Indeed, it may be asserted that, inasmuch as the study of the defects of the blind, the deaf mute and the idiotic has resulted in the discovery of some of the most valuable axioms of educational science, so will the steady, careful and masterly training of the criminal add other axioms equally valuable in a complete system of education. Indeed, there is a distinct department of pedagogics which has received hardly any attention, that which relates to the art of training how to unlearn. This is done by all sane human beings and usually goes by the name of experience, but what the nature is of the psychological process, or to what extent it may be availed of for purposes of metamorphosing bad habits into good has yet to be gathered and formulated into educational axioms.

Family System.—In this field, it is not premature to say that the family system of discipline for penal institutions must take an important place, especially for the young in Reformatories. It enables the managers, by a skilful selection of temperaments and dispositions which shall healthfully react on each other, to segregate those who suffer from similar deficiencies, so that the defects of one shall not become a demoralizing example to the rest, and to group such natures as present well-organized habits so as to become exemplars to those who lack those special habits, thus to consciously organize, by artificial means, an environment in which the convicts themselves will become instruments for each other's regeneration. The present deplorable condition of the prison system in our State justifies the question : Shall the Elmira Reformatory be this opportunity and become a new departure, or be a base repetition of the present failure ? It has been said that the family system is, after all, a modification of the congregate. This criticism is equal to that of the man who said, when looking at a beautifully modeled statue, made in clay taken from the road which he had traveled to visit the artist's studio : " Well, after all, this is only the mud I trod on." The point is not the material, but the use that is made of it ; and if the family system is admitted to be a modification of the congregate, the difference between them is the difference between mud and art.

INDEX.